Applause from Professional Speakers and Consultants

"This new book is a gem among the available resources of making money as a speaker/trainer. Dennis's many years of experience gives him valuable insights into the healthcare and speaking industries. He has put together a wealth of information in a step-by-step easy to read format. He addresses details and topics that newbies would probably not think of, and he does it in a way that is motivating and not intimidating. These are tips and nuggets that will translate into higher profits."

Barbara Augello, MS, EMT-B
healthednewnengland.com

"Dennis Mahoney is at the top of his profession in health care speaking and consulting, so there's no one better to tell you the secrets that will make your business successful too. This book is filled with practical tips and advice that will transform the way you think about your opportunities as a health care expert, helping you translate your expertise into something your clients and prospects really value and want to pay for."

– Suzanne Bates, CSP
www.bates-communications.com

"This book is a practical guide, step-by-step toolkit, and motivational read all rolled into one. For the healthcare professional that is serious about starting a speaking/consulting business, you'll find everything that you need to know in here from an expert who has done it himself."

Elizabeth Freedman, MBA
elizabethfreedman.com

"When I was younger my mother told me to take the best qualities of people I meet and make them my own. When it comes to Dennis and teaching I'm still taking" this book is very informative and well written."

Lt. Tom Labelle
cprbrockton.com

"I had the opportunity to engage Dennis as the keynote speaker for a new healthcare company. The staff was universal in its praises of the leadership Dennis exhibited and the insights he shared for a company in its infancy. He took us from "storming"' to norming. His facts were presented in such a manner that it encouraged feedback and participation. People were able to let down their guard and not feel vulnerable."

- Doyle Moore
Correctional Healthcare Expert

"Motivational, inspirational, and filled with great information. Dennis takes you through the steps to become a great professional speaker in the healthcare industry. His passion and enthusiasm makes this a fun and easy read. This is the only book you will ever need to learn how to grow your speaking career."

- Jacki Rose,
Jackirose.com

"Dennis Mahoney has written the most comprehensive and practical guide for healthcare professionals who truly want to Speak and Consult. Based on over thirty years of knowledge and experience he takes you through the steps that will turn your vision into reality."

- Don Saracen
Strategiesatwork.com

" Dennis truly has a pulse on healthcare speaking. His new book is a 'healthcare speaking plan' that is a prescription for speaking and consulting success. Take one chapter daily as needed for an improved speaking and consulting practice."

-Mache Seibel, MD aka DocRock
Founder, healthrock.com

"A how to book guiding the reader on how to start a successful speaking and consulting practice, written by an experienced speaker who walks the talk. Kit's an easy read, honest and enjoyable with hundreds if practice al tips and many exercises to make your learning a pleasure. A great buy for anyone excited about professionals speaking and consulting." Thank you Dennis.

-Steve Shama, M.D,
Steveshama.com

"Dennis Mahoney is the one mentor who helped me clarify what business options will give me the greatest profit, while building on my existing products and area of expertise. He not only points the way, but identifies concrete do-able steps and suggests proven resources to make those steps cost effective. The end result is a new workable plan for business growth and increased profit. Dennis' down-to-earth, humorous style coupled with his business acumen makes him a mentor you want to have by your side." Thank you so much Dennis!

Linda Varone, R.N., M.A.
thesmarthomeoffice.com

Make Money as a Consultant And Speaker in Healthcare"

"A Step by Step System
To Build, Market and Grow
A Profitable
Consulting and Speaking Business"

By

Dennis C. Mahoney, MPH, CSP

A FALLON PRESS BOOK

Second printing October 2011

ISBN printed edition: **978-0-9824556-0-9**

Visit our web site – www.dennismahoney.org

Contact: dennis@dennismahoney.org

1-617-298-0699

CONTENTS

Preface

A recent USA Today/Gallop poll reported that over 25% of all working adults want to start their own full or part-time business and millions more would like to dabble in side projects in order to earn more money.

Have you wanted to start you own business and earn extra money, be your own boss, control your work schedule, give yourself a raise, or design your perfect job description?

Have you thought about providing your healthcare expertise through consulting, coaching, training or speaking professionally?

If so, this book is for you.

If you are like me, you have probably experienced that inner voice screaming out to you to start your own full or part-time professional practice.

One late winter night years ago, I was watching the late night interview talk show hosted by Tom Snyder. Not only was Tom a unique and gifted interviewer, but he always had exceptional and different guests on his show. That night Richard Bolles – author of the book *"What Color is Your Parachute"* was on Tom's show. Bolles book was written to help people change careers. I was instantly impressed and excited about his unique approach to career change. I went out the next day, bought the book, completed the exercises in the book, and quit my job two weeks later. It was the last time I ever worked in an organization on a full-time basis.

I don't think there ever was a time in my career in healthcare that I hadn't been bending somebody's ear about either how I was going to start my own professional business or how they should start their own business. I had worked as in acute care, served as a hospital department manager, medical university faculty member, clinical instructor, behavioral counselor, and preventive medicine expert.

During all those fulfilling and admirable roles, I was still investigating the possibility of starting a speaking and training business. I might even take a few baby steps into the entrepreneurial world with small and part-time speaking or consulting projects.

It seemed like I was always in the "idea" or "planning" stage of one dream job or another. I was always going to look into one or another resource that would instantly skyrocket me into success.

After watching Tom Snyder's show, some divine intervention, professional mentoring, and a lot of work, I finally jumped into action. I committed to building and promoting a successful speaking and consulting practice.

As a professional healthcare speaker and consultant and following a process I developed, I was able to:

- Function as a consultant and successfully earn over one million dollars from grants in government, non-profit associations, and education.
- Develop a successful training business
- Present speeches to over forty thousand healthcare professionals.

Throughout those years not only did I find out I love to provide presentations and services to my audiences and clients but also that that I am an expert in designing processes, assessments, lists and charts – total systems.

It is with that passion and expertise that I wrote this book for you. I am excited about sharing with you an efficient and effective system that will support you in growing your own healthcare practice.

Introduction

Over sixty years ago the New York police arrested a famous bank robber by the name of Willie Sutton. When they took Willie to the police station and interrogated him, a reporter asked Willie, "Willie – why do you rob banks?" He simply answered – "because that's where the money is."

The key benefits of professional speaking and consulting in healthcare are not only about finding out where the money is and earning fees, but also:

- Earning praise from the expert information that also gives you a sense of fulfillment
- Providing critical solutions and vision for your audiences and clients
- Earning passive income from your intellectual properties – books, CD's, e-books, webinars, etc...

Every day there are hundreds of thousands of meetings and conferences in the United States. Many of these meetings require a main speaker (keynote) for anywhere from 100 – 1000 attendees, and many additional speakers to lead smaller group sessions (breakout or workshop sessions) of 20-100 attendees. There are multiple opportunities for you at these meetings.

There are thousands of healthcare facilities, practices, service organizations and associations short and long term consultants at an average daily rate of $1000.00.

The top three growing industries in the United States are education, government, and healthcare. Over two trillion dollars or 16 percent of the gross national product are spent in healthcare. That is to say one out of every six dollars is spent in the healthcare industry in the United States.

Professional Speakers are paid for presenting information to those who value improving their productivity and/or profitability. Success is measured in outcomes accomplished from your audiences. Your goals as a professional speaker are to eliminate barriers to your message by providing your information in a clear, accurate, appropriate manner and always giving your audience or client more than they expect. For example after your presentation, you might provide a free half hour phone consultation, or provide a free assessment tool or copy of you latest publication.

Your speaking may allow you to:

- Deliver a keynote speech
- Teach a break-out sessions
- Facilitate workshops
- Sponsor a series of training leading to professional credentialing
- Speak at webinars or tele-conferences

Consulting is a profession in which you ask the right questions of your clients and provide them with solutions based on your expertise and experience.

Writing is also available to you in order to *leverage* your intellectual properties in the form of books, manuals, e-books, tips books, audio programs, video formats, and many more web based opportunities

Whether your specialty is management, administration, finance, preventive medicine, holistic health, critical care, adult learning, nutrition, fitness, diabetes, medical care, supervision, or patient satisfaction, there are many clients and audiences waiting for you.

Whether you are a senior administrator, manager, nurse, allied health professional, social worker, behavioral health counselor, personal fitness trainer, or any other healthcare professional, this book is especially for you. Speaking and consulting opportunities addressing healthcare issues exist in corporate America as well as healthcare associations, agencies and medical practices.

Your expertise can transfer to the many healthcare market segments and you will be able to build a profitable practice of speaking and consulting in healthcare.

The information in this book was developed to take you from "dreaming' about a profitable part or full time healthcare consulting and speaking practice to becoming that successful entrepreneur.

The chapters will guide you through the following eight steps. Each chapter and topic includes tips, easy "how to" steps, assessments, application tools, case studies and summaries.

My systematic approach will inspire, teach, and help you to build, market, and grow your healthcare consulting and speaking practice.

You will learn how to:

- Discover your passion, and willingness to speak.
- Identify your ability to market your unique expertise.
- Find those who will pay for your expert information.
- Write and present effective and exciting content.
- Present and leverage your knowledge and expertise in numerous venues and formats.
- Organize an efficient and profitable speaking practice.
- Successfully sell services and informational products to your audiences and clients.
- Learn how to maximize the growth of your professional career.

So let's get started. Have fun. Enjoy the journey. This is going to be an exciting adventure in a new phase of your professional life.

Journey On

So, here you are. You can't wait to start your speaking and consulting business. You are highly passionate about what you perceive as your unique expertise.

Where do you start?

The first step is to be very clear on **why** you are going to build your business around that passion and expertise.

One of the most common mistakes of people wanting to success at their business is not answering the following questions:

- What are your professional visions?
- What are your personal visions?
- What size or scope do you want your business to attain?
- What model will you design?
- What will be your niche market?
- What presentations and products will serve as the core for your business? How do you want to be spending your time?

To sustain any energy and overcome the obstacles to your success you must deal with this "willingness" issue.

In my experience as a coach, trainer and speaker to aspiring speakers, trainers and consultants, I have discovered that to first define and maintain one's willingness, to build a speaking and consulting practice.

Fulfill Your Purpose

Are you excited, enthused, and passionate about your expertise?

Do you have a burning need to fulfill that special purpose in life?

Do you toss and turn at night in bed thinking and wishing you could take a different direction in your professional life?

Do you want to be known by the message you want to deliver to the world?

If the answers to all the above questions are yes, then you are well on your way to becoming profitable as a professional speaker.

Look at your new career as a candy store: so much opportunity, so many choices but where do you start, where do you focus?

What is it you really want from your new career? Is it fame, fortune, travel, adulation, or social accomplishments? Helping people and healthcare organizations

This is your opportunity to sculpture the perfect job and lifestyle for yourself.

How can you make a difference? This should be the essence of your professional life. You will only be able to grow your business if you are highly motivated and passionate about your topic(s) and your audiences. Stay focused and vigilant on the purpose that drives you to become a professional speaker. Set purposeful business goals based on that motivation driven by your passion.

This book will help you find that perfect audience and client that needs your special and unique expertise.

With passion as your "engine", your chance of profit and accomplishing your strategic outcomes increases tremendously. To confirm your level of passion for your goals, answer these questions

What is a purpose, issue or topic that keeps you awake at night?

_____

_____

What were you most interested as a child? _____

_____

Why do you want to get your message out to others?

_____

_____

_____

If you were not paid what would you still speak about, that would have a purpose and meaning?

_____

_____

_____

What gave you the greatest sense of joy and accomplishment in your career thus far? _____

_____

_____

What do you value as the most important outcome or mission when you speak to groups? _____

_____

The highest level on *Maslow's Hierarchy of Needs* is termed "self-actualization". The second highest level includes self-esteem, confidence, achievement, respect of others, and respect by others.

The need for fulfilling a social purpose is core to us as social beings. This usually is comparatively easy for those working in the helping professions. Who do you want to help with your expertise? What do you want your image to be? What do you want to be known as an expert on?

We only have to look to *Maslow's Hierarchy of Needs* to help confirm what we know to be our purpose for starting a speaking and consulting business.

Motivation is Easy

One definition in the dictionary of *lazy is "without motivation"*.

The definition of motivation is *provide with an incentive and move to action*.

It is important to identify the benefits that will keep you motivated. .

Big Benefits

Hopefully this book has raised your enthusiasm and passion towards sharing your expertise and developing your own business. The common benefits for professional speakers and consultants usually fall into two categories, and are as follows:

1. "What's the payoff" – what's in it for you?

    a) Money
    b) Fulfillment
    c) Receiving positive feedback and praise
    d) Meeting your personal or professional needs

2. <u>What will others think of you</u> – either because you accomplish or fail at a task:

    a. Reward
    b. Praise
    c. Scorn
    d. Punishment
    e. Ambivalence

List Your Benefits

How do these reasons and benefits rate with you?

Benefits	Your score lowest (1-10) highest
Pursue your passion	
Provide your expertise to those in need	
Have fun and be fulfilled with your work	
Control your own work schedule	
Decide a design the scope of your business	
Control over your earning ability	
Paid travel (by client and/or tax deduction	
Have fun and be fulfilled with your work	

Have fun and be fulfilled with your work	
Earn praise and recognition from colleagues, clients and audiences	
TOTAL =	
Did you score 100?	

How do you know you are willing?

You have acquired an enormous amount of specialized knowledge and are functioning at a very high level with a unique mix of skills. There are many healthcare businesses and organizations that could benefit from your expertise.

Levels of Willingness Questionnaire

Circle the number below for each question. Add the circled numbers. Compare your score below

On a scale of one to six (six being highest)

1	2	3	4	5	6

a. How likely will it be that you will agree to spend up to $5000.00 within the next three months, towards starting your practice?

1	2	3	4	5	6

b. How important is it that your business be speaking and/or consulting?

----

1   2   3   4   5   6

c.   How much support do you have from your household members?

----

1   .   2   3   4   5   6

d.   How strong is the urge to start your own business?

----

1   2   3   4   5   6

e.   Do people tell you this is what you should be doing?

----

1   2   3   4   5   6

f.   Are you willing to put in the work that it takes to stand out in your expert niche?

----

1   2   3   4   5   6

g.   How much do you believe that you will be in business (either part-or full tie) by this time next year?

What is your level of Willingness?

If your score was below (7 – 13) - reassess your life goals, too many barriers

If your score was (14-20) –your passion is stable, maybe you need to choose another one of your areas of expertise

If your score was (21-30) - you are highly, but need to identify and deal with potential barriers

If your score was (31-40) you are on fire and ready to go!

Committing to Willingness

In order to be willing to commit to being a professional speaker, you must assess what is and what will be important to you in all roles of your life.

Commitment Appraisal Tool

First fill in the blanks with how much time you need for each area of your life. Then, on a scale of 1-10 (1 being the lowest value, 10 being the highest value),

1. I need _____ (minutes per day) of personal "alone" time
2. I need _____ (hours or days) of family time.
3. I need _____ days of time to be involved in community and civic activities per month.
4. I need _____ days of recreational time per month.
5. I need _____ free time to socialize
6. I only want to travel _____ days a month.
7. I need energy and _____ time for my avocation(s)
8. I need $ _____ and _____ time for my other ventures

Assign a value to the eight factors. Assess which above need is a must for your new lifestyle when you design your business model.

Divide the list into thirds, (1/3 – most important, 1/3 somewhat important, and least important)

1._____   2._____   3._____   4._____

5._____   6._____   7._____   8._____

Obstacles to Maintaining Your Willingness

Years ago (am I'm dating myself), when there was an army draft in this country, a good friend of mine received his draft notice. His famous comment upon receiving his notice was "This comes at a bad time."

When is there a good time to do anything especially if it involves work?

Generally people, places, and things get in our way of our goals.

Avoiding Negativity

Surround yourself with only supportive and positive people. Get rid of that baggage.

- Life- it gets in the way. Stay focused and have a daily plan of small tasks to accomplish – remember – "how you eat an elephant – one bite at a time".
- Mental programming - One has to be willing (and able) to be successful in anything we do. If you tell yourself, "I can," or "I can't," that usually will be the answer.
- Discipline impacts on motivation and can be broken down into a few simple directives:
  - o If you stay motivated, and with a little skill in staying focused, you will be well disciplined
  - o The secrets to being disciplined are:
    - Be passionate about your goals
    - Care about your audiences and clients
    - Have fun with your work (output)

The good news and bad news is that our habits and emotions are the culprits. The occurrence of these two factors is very random and mostly uncontrollable. If they were controllable and predictable life would be very boring. How we deal with them is totally controllable.

Usually the biggest barriers are generated from ourselves. It is not the outside world. The most common other than us are:

The common results of bad habits and not dealing with emotional cues are:

Lack of:

- Passion
- Purpose
- Appropriate level of expertise
- Commitment
- Focus
- Planning
- Vision of scope of business

We are all motivated by any one or combination of fame, fortune, family or social status. Which applies to you?

Although going through the process for myself took me a number of hours, I was able to confirm with one hundred percent certainty every task that I did, and didn't want to do. I was also able to write my perfect speaking practice "career and lifestyle" description.

Strategies to Maintain Your Willingness

I have listed a few suggestions for you to help you foster your enthusiasm, passion and motivation.

- Remind yourself daily, why you are passionate about pursuing a specific purpose in life
- Review your personal benefits daily.

- Have fun and be fulfilled by developing and delivering your services and products
- ~~Constantly remind yourself about your need to control your own professional activities~~
- Anticipate and deal frequent obstacles.
- Commit to frequently evaluate the implementation of your strategies and goals of your business plan

Assessing Your Ability

Recently I was talking with a speech therapist who has worked with elementary school children for over 20 years. She was ready to retire from the school system where she worked. She was very proud of her ability to design unique and exceptional developmental activities for the multi-handicapped student.

When I asked her if she has considered starting a speaking and consulting business built around these unique materials and activities she replied "there really is no market for them because all my colleagues are at the same level and also know how to create these same games and tools."

I suggested to her that she might consider that her target audience could be the parents of children with speech issues. Wouldn't they love to learn the fundamentals, principles and techniques, in using or developing these speech games after school in order to help their own children? That really opened up her eyes (and mine) to the possibilities.

Credentials and qualifications are relative. There is always a very particular client or audience who needs and wants only you. She is very passionate about changing the lives of the children, and now she can change those lives directly through the family. Isn't that a great thing to be known for?

She had a deep passion and caring for not only the children but was also very excited and enthusiastic and designing even more of her unique materials for speech improvement.

 She has decided to consider consulting and speaking as a part time or full time role. Her main drive in the process is passion, a purpose in life. She has found hers.

- Identify your expertise and specialty niche
- Assess your ability to provide specific expertise
- Design the professional and personal lifestyle you desire
- Write the exact mission and vision statements for your professionals activities
- Begin to narrow the niche and market for your business
- Initiate building a brand and image for your business

Let's start by inventory your formal and informal education. You will be tempted to skip this step. You will say to yourself, "I know what I want to do and know what I am good at." This might be the most important step in the whole book.

Perhaps you have some non-health related or non-professional expertise that you have. What kinds of activities have you always enjoyed, even as a child? What kinds of tasks and projects do you find yourself attracted to?

Career Appraisal Tool

I develop the following exercise to initially identify my speaking career. I re-assess my speaking and consulting career about every five years and still use this method. I know you will find this very helpful towards defining your unique expertise and niche market.

For this exercise you will need paper, four different colored pens, and a pack of index cards.

Steps:

1. Title a separate sheet of paper with each separate professional credential that you hold. List all formal education, continuing education, certifications, and licenses, awards, accomplishments, etc…
2. For each of the credentials, write a general description and list all the tasks that have earned with your credentials.
3. One credential at a time, with the first colored pen – circle all the tasks you absolutely do not want to ever perform again.
4. Now with the second colored pen, circle the tasks might be needed to be performed in your new practice, but you will delegate.
5. Next with the third colored pen circle the tasks that you will do, but which are not rewarding.
6. Circle the tasks with the fourth colored pen that you love to do.
7. List the five top talents that people tell you that you excel on separate index cards.
8. Describe the characteristics of the ideal clients or audiences, and venues you would like to spend your time.
9. Write descriptions of the ideal clients or audiences, and venues you would **not** like to spend your time.
10. List each of the circled items you love to do from each credential list on each separate index cards.
11. On each index card describe each venue in detail.
12. On each separate card write each ideal client.
13. Now randomly arrange on a table top, only the cards from steps 5 – 8 and prioritize and combine your top five tasks.

Now for the fun – In your own style or approach,
- Combine your favorite tasks
- Desirable audience types
- Desired venues
- Thing people tell you that you are good at doing
- Functions you will need to do to manage your practice.

Combine all these factors into a prose statement. This will be a very specific and descriptive statement that can be reviewed periodically to reconfirm and review your expertise and niche.

Declare Your Niche

If you focus on one group of individuals, organizations, or professions, you will reach success faster and more effectively. Stick to what you know.

What do you want to be known for? What will be your value in the marketplace?

You are now ready to that perfect niche. What are you an expert at and what makes you unique? Choose the top group or client or audience (market) from your "speaking career and lifestyle summary statement" description. This market and the specific expertise (topic) you have prioritized is your initial niche.

In order to be an expert, you don't have to the number one expert only a good expert to your focused niche.

My unique expertise is:

_____

_____

_____

My marketable skills and knowledge are:

_____

_____
_____

I would prefer to speak and consult to audiences and clients with the characteristics and profiles of:

_____

_____ _____

The work conditions I prefer are:

_____

_____
_____

The work conditions I will not accept are:

_____

_____

_____

_____
_____

When and where do I want to speak?

_____

_____

_____

I would like to be known for (and as):

_____

_____

I would describe (characterize) my key target markets as: _____

_____

_____

 It may sound a little morbid, but a good trick to write your bio sketch is to write it as if it were your obituary. Consider what you have accomplished, and what else you would like to do and be known for the rest of your life. This can serve as an additional source in defining your direction and writing your business plan.   Including all the questions in the above sections, write that perfect description of your speaking and consulting practice.

Embrace Success

People classically get stuck in the "thinking or "investigative" step of their dreams and goals because of the fear of succeeding. Sub-consciously they process the fear of actually getting what they want and then believe they can't handle the responsibility, stress, and new expectations.

Don't be afraid of success. Stay focused on your dreams and goals, along with an effective market analysis, they will happen. Dale Carnegie said, "80 percent of what we worry about never happens." That is so true. The biggest reason we do not accomplish our life goals is that we are afraid of success. Yes, afraid of success not failure. Many people are afraid of even successful change. With success come perceived responsibility, stress, increased workload, and new relationships. Unscheduled change is traumatic and stressful. The more we can control our destiny or at the least be aware of where we are going, the less stress there will be. Change is scary. As human beings, although we will deal with it, we don't like change, especially when we see it as confrontation. Some additional fears you may have are: fear of debt, lack of business, and too much work. All of these are scary conditions to us.

Although we, in the helping professions lean towards the altruistic purpose in all we do, capitalism in our democratic society is a noble cause. Moving from non-profit to a for-profit business may be a cultural change for you.

Change can be a challenge whether it is desired or not. There is never a good time for many situations in life. Too many times we block our readiness to act because of fear. It is natural to balk at new adventures in our lives. Keep moving from "no" to a fired up, "Yes!" Just like

that little Engine that we all read about when we were young, you can do it.

Don't let fear deter you from your dreams. You may be presently very unhappy where you are working now. The leading causes of stress, anxiety dissatisfaction, and depression in the workplace are aggravating fellow employees who don't carry their fair share, unreasonable managers and bosses, and over -whelming workloads. Don't let the present or past influence your future!

The path of least resistance is natural from the small amoeba to all human beings. Embrace change. Embrace challenges. This really is what life is all about. These are the things that keep us alive. Some of the secrets to enjoying your business are to: 1) Plan the work and then work the plan and 2) Work the plan and do it in baby steps. My sainted mother's advice to me was, "If you count your pennies, the dollars will take care of themselves." Go for it, don't worry, carpe diem.

Don't fail because of something you didn't do. Later is now.

In your speaking and consulting business these additional skills, habits and routines will support your purpose and passion:

- Remain focused
- "eat that elephant – one bite at a time"
- Stay organized
- Develop relevant material
- Present quality content
- Promote yourself consistently

As you perform the above even for 3-6 hours a day, and perform these in an organized and efficient process you will become and remain a success.

Zero in on Your Niche

You will need to match your level of expertise to the appropriate level of client and audience. Complete the assessment tools in this chapter to identify the best expert area to start out with.

Your level of expertise is a relative thing. In the United States alone there are 340 million people. An equation to solve for your business to becoming successful is:

 # (number of clients) x $$ (fees) = Desired Lifestyle

No matter what your level of expertise – there is a market out there for you. What services and informational products can you contribute to the healthcare system?

A huge golden rule as you move into your new career is to never compare yourself to anyone with a lesser or better reputation or size of business than you. Strive to be the best, and be competitive in the market. Personalizing professional competition will only serve as a barrier to success.

You probably will not be able to be the star quarterback in the next Super Bowl, or the next President of the United States. I gave up a long time ago trying to be a brain surgeon or nuclear physicist.

You definitely have competencies that qualify you as an expert to a client or audience somewhere. With your unique background, you are the top expert to a group somewhere. Start out with your most passionate and deepest area, and evolve from there. Although the chapters follow a linear step by step system, you are able to focus on a set of competencies as you desire. The outcome will result in you standing out in your niche and expertise areas.

As you recall the *speech therapist* I mentioned earlier, had a good target market. She felt she was exceptional in developing the developmentally appropriate activities for her kindergarten students to improve their speech. She also felt that most of her colleagues already had the same level of expertise and ability to develop similar activities. She was correct. I suggested to her that the parents of those children didn't possess that skill, and she could market her activities to the parents to use after school, at home with the kids, to additionally work with their speech improvement.

How many levels can you be an expert and to whom? Who will pay you the fees you require for that expertise?

Speak on what you:

- Do currently as a job
- Are perceived as an expert
- Are passionate about

I have added this bonus for you to help you explore opportunities in the healthcare industry.

The following chart is for you to consider one or more specific components of the continuum of healthcare model. The model was developed by Donald Vickery, M.D. There are a number of possibilities to choose as a niche.

Steps of Continuum of Care in Healthcare	What could you provide?
• Newborn to Adult specialty	
• Self-Care Education	
• Lifestyle Case Management	
• Targeted Interventions	
• Self-study	
• Medical Self-Care	
• Primary Care	
• Emergency Care	
• Chronic Disease Management	
• Hospitalization/Surgery	
• Case Management	
• Hospice	

You might also consider using the prevention model to brainstorm more possibilities in developing your niche area. The table below includes the top seven causes of adult deaths in the United States per year. In the chart on the next page check off the disease and level of prevention that might be a niche for you.

Primary Level of Prevention

Empowerment of individuals, families, and communities to achieve and maintain their maximal health and functioning through promotion of health enhancing behaviors and the reduction of biological, economic, social, and environmental risk factors which contribute to the incidence of illness and health problems and disability.

Secondary Level of Prevention

Early detection and intervention to promote the health and well-being of those who are at most risk of illness, or are beginning to experience health related problems and disabilities.

Tertiary Level of Prevention

Treatment to promote the maximal health of those experiencing illness or injury designed to limit further disability and secondary conditions resulting from the initial health problem

Cause of Death	Primary Prevention	Secondary Prevention	Tertiary Prevention
Heart Disease			
Cancer			
Stroke			
COPD			
Diabetes			
Injuries			
Infections			

If you combine the tenets of the Continuum of Care model, the three levels of prevention, sub specialties of healthcare management education or research, and delivery systems of healthcare, (treatment sites, networks, agencies, and associations) you now have an infinite number of options for your niche, expertise and market.

List the Most Important Benefits to You

You will only become a financially successful professional speaker if you see what is in it for you. Make a list of the key benefits you value. Keep this posted over your computer and on your bathroom mirror. The benefit might be more time traveling with the family on vacations, coaching your child's little league team, paying off some of those credit cards or increasing your visibility within your profession. Look at it every day and let the list support your passion and motivation. Develop a sense of urgency – it always motivates.

I still have mine own hanging on a bulletin board right above my computer. I printed it out in 18 pt. font size and put it in a plastic sheet protector. I keep it to remind me how blessed I am to have been such a successful speaker all these years.

Developing a Speaking Practice

Constantly remind yourself about the payoff(s). What benefit excites you when you dream of having a profitable business? What allows you to remain in healthcare? Is it money, adulation, control of your own destiny, managing your own business or all the above? What is your dream job? What do you dream about doing when you are at work? What do you Google? What do you always talk to your friends about that you would like to do someday?

Life is not a dress rehearsal – do it now!

We are motivated to act by a number of factors:

1) Recognition
2) Reward
3) Avoiding unpleasant consequences
3) Mandated
2) Financial
3) Inner drive for accomplishment
4) Social impacts and expectations
6) Biological satisfaction
7) Most important for us as speakers, fulfilling one's
   Purpose in life

How Will Speaking Impact Your Personal Life?

_____

_____

Does your written answer match your dreams?

The whole purpose of becoming a healthcare professional speaker is to fully enjoy what you do and provide help for those who need your expertise. Write an "ideal lifestyle" statement. This will be a fun exercise and step in your plan. Complete the exercise to see what your ideal lifestyle might look like.

 If you have identified your most passionate expertise, stay focused and let nothing interfere with acquiring the lifestyle you desire, and then you will find a fun and fulfilling life waiting for you very soon. Determine where you want to work. Map out your ideal day, week, or month.

Now put your plan in a prose format. Hang it up to see every day. Do not alter. Stick to it. Get on with developing and promoting your content.

Write Your Mission and Vision Statements

To succeed long term, you must feel you are fulfilling a purpose or mission. To plan for the future requires vision. In order to be clear or have clarity, one must write out your mission and vision as statements.

Be sure to include your unique values that you provide, in both statements.

Develop and communicate your vision so that it aligns with your client and audiences.

A **mission statement** describes who you are. This is part of the real pay-off for owning your own practice. You are able to construct a descriptive statement for your business that includes your personal values, beliefs, and societal and personal goals. Ideally this statement should be brief, and to the point.

Questions to answer in a mission statement:
- What are your values and philosophy?
- What are your basic professional needs that you need to fulfill or address?
- What competencies, skills, methods, and systems do you use in your business?
- Who are your clients and audiences?
- What makes you unique? What distinguishes you from other speakers and consultants?

Your mission statement should be **value driven.**

Write a **vision statement** describing where you are going. In this statement you can refer to a long term plan, but it is better to address the outcomes you wish to achieve within the next three to five years. I emphasize this because my observations and experiences have been that changes (for many reasons) can totally take you down another direction in your business scope and desires. By setting your vision realistically, you will be able and willing to adapt to change easier.

In establishing clear (fairly permanent) written statements you establish a set of guidelines that will serve as your litmus test to every business decision and question you will need answered.

It is Time to Buy Your Domain Names

This step might seem a little out of place. At this point, if you are convinced that you want to speak and consult professionally, then you are going to have to promote yourself. Domain names are those

names that we use to introduce ourselves to our markets on the internet. Over the next few months you will find yourself buying and owning a number of domain names. The first one(s) you need to own are your own name with the .com, and/or .org, and/or .net, and/or .us. Just Google - - "domain names." Your search will discover a number of vendors approved to assist you buying and owning your domain names.

So run - don't walk and buy your domain name now! Your domain name will be your key brand. If it is not available try grabit.com

What key words do people use to find your particular healthcare expertise? Use those to create a name.

Your core identity in the marketplace as a professional speaker is your name. You may elect to operate under any number of other names or themes, but your name is core. Hopefully no one has "bought" your name yet.

There are providers on the internet that will license your name and validate that it belongs to you. There is whois.com. and many others. I prefer godaddy.com they are established and provide all the services

and features you will need for your web site. They are also priced well below many other providers. I have had good luck with them. I do not receive any reimbursement for this endorsement, only good service. Ideally you want to buy your domain name in com, net, org, and misspelling.

Preliminary Connect Outline

Define and list the "general" sub-topics and formats that you would like to develop. This information will serve as the foundation for your survey and market assessment processes.

Chapter Two

Don't Guess Assess

Finding Your Market

"Meet their needs and they will meet yours"

Dennis Mahoney

These are the key functions in building your business. If you correctly conduct a market analysis you cannot fail. You will be successful. You will meet your goals. If you don't conduct a market analysis there is a 90 percent chance you will fail.

Most practitioners do not perform a legitimate market analysis because:

1) They don't want to find out there is no market for their expertise
2) They are so enthused about their personal bias and opinion on the value of their topic and expertise that they steam ahead, or
3) They are impatient and can't wait to develop and promote their expertise and information.

Don't get caught in this trap Perform an effective market analysis.

Your goal is to identify the narrowest niche for a particular market that will support your financial and personal life goals. Don't be that kid in the candy store that wants everything they see. Pick one, focus, and finish the project before you move on to the next.

Correctly assessing and diagnosing a situation is the highest of skills in any professional field. The successes of all interventions, plans, and outcomes are proportionally based on the quality of your assessment.

In order to meet the expectations of your audiences and clients, you must know what they want. The best technique to find out what they want is to ask them directly.

It seems like a basic and simple concept – right? Well, guess what the number one reason people fail in their speaking business is? You guessed it – incorrectly assuming what their clients or audiences need.

By conducting an effective market analysis you will meet 100 percent of the audiences' and clients' expectations.

Years ago I sponsored public seminars on critical care medicine. We sponsored eight full day programs a month in major cities in the United States. Our average attendance was 50 – 100 attendees. Most were registered nurses, physicians, respiratory and physical therapists. For one particular program, I reserved meeting space, printed over 5000 brochures, paid postage to send out those brochures and contracted with five speakers to join me for a daylong seminar, and promoted the workshop by direct mail. I should have received at least one percent of responses back for registrations (50 participants). I received none. The seminar topic was "How to Deal With the Sexuality of the Acute Care Patient." This program was targeted for critical care personnel, particularly registered nurses. I relied on one person, a friend who was doing her thesis on aspects of sexuality with hospitalized patients for my "market analysis." She was passionate about the topic but no one else was. At that time in our culture, no one else valued that topic area. I learned an expensive lesson. Get your guidance from the horse's mouth.

Unsuccessful speakers "marry" their topic so closely that they are afraid of hearing that it is not needed or wanted. If you are in the correct niche, and possess a unique expertise, your audiences and clients will direct you to the correct specific approach they would like to learn. Have faith.

More than likely your market analysis will validate what you hoped would be the need.

As you develop and implement your market analysis, be very objective, recruit other professionals to help you interpret the data, and develop a process that will serve as a continuous surveying and validating process.

Before you get started, review the characterizations of your key target market(s) so it is fresh in your mind. Zero in on those images for your initial research.

All the information you obtain from your market research or market analysis is classified into three categories

1) Primary Data - The information collected specifically for the purpose of the research project at hand. What did the respondents say they wanted exactly and/or what else would they buy?
2) Secondary data – the information collected from many valid and numerous related sources i.e. – literature, colleagues, science, standards of practice, etc…
3) Trend data - Where and what are the current and future **documented** trends?

All the data sources are measured by numbers (quantitative) or by a standard (qualitative).

I consistently look at the assessment process as if I'm throwing a pebble in a pond. I think of individuals as being those inner ripples, the primary data, and then moving towards the outer ripples – the secondary data. I systematically work my way from the most intimate sources and information (client or audience) to the more general (industry etc...)

This chart below will help you start your market analysis process. How many more sources can you think to add to this chart?

Sample Market Analysis Source Chart

professional Journal list	professional articles
e-mail list	research and Studies
postal mail list	medsearch.com
association lists	individual Interviews
meeting planners	focus Groups
factfinder.census.gov	other Speakers and Consultants
directories	government resources, data
client input	primary, secondary data
professional web sites	competitors
science	industry standards of practice
credentialing guidelines	written surveys
electronic surveys	grant sources

An important survey source is the government. Explore additional federal, state and local laws, ordinances and compliances that apply to healthcare organizations. Search the Federal Information Center (FIC) for a directory of the billions of dollars and research documents available free of charge for you.

Check out the Request for Proposals (RFP) that the government agencies might have out to bid. Although cities and states have the biggest budgets of any businesses, they don't maintain employees. They hire consultants and sub-contractors. Meet with your legislator and/or their staffers. You are their constituent and a tax payer. The job they want to do is to help you.

You can also meet with grantors of non-governmental fund sources. There are more than 71,000 grants making foundations and nearly 900,000 nonprofit organizations giving away over 40 billion dollars a year. Everyone thinks that it is illegal or unethical to approach the grantor. It is not. They want you to meet the requests of their proposal (that's why they call them "request for proposals- RFP). They want you to answer the questions in the RFP so they can determine if you are going to meet their expectations and deliver the outcomes (deliverables). Their organizations have a mission and need you to provide the services to meet their ends. The best way to accomplish this is to meet and interview them face to face.

Is There a Market for Your Message?

Do what you know best. If your background is the healthcare industry, then the best niche area for you to be successful is healthcare.

Think about what group has an interrelated set of interests. How they are alike and what do they want as a group? What do you have that matches their needs?

That is not to say that if your background is finance that you can't bridge into another industry where your base skills are applicable. You could, for example, use your healthcare background in geriatrics to move into any one of the retirement industries (housing, recreation, travel, and wellness.) A colleague of mine used her geriatric rehabilitation experiences to speak to senior groups about activities to keep the body and mind stimulated after retirement. She plans to build her entire business model around this topic.

At this point in the process you don't have to be specific regarding your topic content or written materials. Relax. Let it flow. As you start to collect your survey information; you will be able to narrow the exact direction and end point that will be your ideal niche.

The Job is Always Easy with the Right Tools

The process needs to be influenced by the best conditions in order to give you the best results

How you design and ask the questions are critical. Who you ask is critical. You have already identified who you want in your audiences and as clients. You will want to survey a representative group from this demographic.

It is also vital that, built into any of the survey formats you determine respondent professional background, attitude towards attending speeches or buying informational products and what they will pay for those services and products. Take your written surveys everywhere. During your survey process, keep one eye on the audiences, and markets you don't want to work with. This is very important.

Ask the Right Question and then Listen

As many parents leave the house to go to work, they are confronted with the following conversation:

Child: "Where are you going?'

Parent: "To work"

Child: "Why?"

Parent: "To earn money"

Child: "Why?"

Parent: "To buy food"

Child: "Why?"

Parent: "So we are all well fed"

Child: "Why?"

And on and on it goes. Children learn very early the best way to obtain information and clarity is to keep asking questions. As adults we lose that instinct and skill. Don't stop just because you are an adult.

There are three considerations for discovering survey information:

- Use interrogatives – what, why, how, where, who and when
- Wait for the answers
- Listen! Don't just hear

Design Your Market Assessment Survey Tools

The two most important communication skills in surveying are listening and asking the right questions.

Who wants your expertise? How do you ask them? How do you reach the potential buyer or group of buyers? Those are not only million dollar questions, but the most important piece of building your business.

The good news is that it is easy. The other good news is that most of your competitors will not go to the trouble of taking this step.

In order to identify who wants what you have to offer you can use many methods of assessing or analyzing the wants and needs of your target markets.

Some traditional methods in healthcare are science base data, trends data, demographics, primary data, and secondary data.

There are essentially five methods to conducting surveys:

1. in person
2. telephone
3. written format
4. electronic format
5. combinations of the above four methods

Don't forget to include yourself in the survey process. The most unanswered question we have as adults for ourselves before or after a behavior is "why." What and how do you like to buy?

One technique I learned that is part of a method used by Alex Mandosian, an informational marketing expert:

1. First establish an "ask" domain. Buy the domain name "ask (plus your first and last name).com." For example I have askdennismahoney.com.
2. Have your web designer set up a page that contains a banner with your head shot and domain name, a text box with the question, "What is your number one most burning question about….(you fill in the rest of the sentence")? The respondent will then answer that "one" question.
3. In another box the respondent will leave their email address and name. Your web designer can arrange to have that email address and their question sent to you in a data collection site.
4. As you collect the questions, you now have a one hundred percent response to what you should develop and deliver to your target audience.

Mandosian used the collected information to develop content for tele-conferences, workshops, etc… this is called leveraging. Leveraging is the process of multiplying the profit from your intellectual properties by offering the information in many formats. The initial format can further be audio-taped to sell, to be given as a free offer or as an additional "leveraged" stream of income for you.

Another technique is written surveys. My book "Women – How to Get Men to Lose Weight" was written by respondents to my survey. I collected over 470 surveys. I asked some demographic information (age, zip code, occupation, gender, race, etc.) then only four questions. The questions were essentially (for women to answer) "Why don't men lose weight or listen to you", and (to the men) "What could women do to help you lose weight and what is it they do that hinders you from losing weight?" I took survey forms everywhere I went, starting with my presentations. I asked other speakers to pass them out at their presentations, at conferences, conventions; everywhere. It only took me five weeks to gather all 470 from over twenty five states. .

One side of the questionnaire was for women to answer and the other side for men to answer. The women told me exactly their experiences and opinions. The men's answers confirmed the women's experiences. I put it all together, researched the science, added gender humor, the latest health trends, and wrote the text.

The questions were general and required brief answers. The responses not only served as the chapters and paragraph headings in the book, but brought to my attention information and sub topics I needed to Include and research further. I also received some good ideas for other publications. The demographics served as statistics peppered throughout the book (i.e. 56 percent of women over 45 year's old living in on the East Coast of the United States)

In developing surveys there can be two considerations.

- Design the tool with no particular person in mind. This format will give you new information and is very objective.
- Or, you can design a format with specific future recipients in mind and how they would accept and use your expertise. This
- will validate your suspicions. Either method or a combination of both can be effective.

Face to Face

Face to face interviews can be effective, especially with no particular person, but a specific sub market group, these can be either one on one or in a focus group format

The key features of facilitating focus groups are:

1. Provide food and refreshments
2. Possible a stipend or gift
3. Prepare written out open-ended questions for yourself to use
4. Set a time limit (one – 2 ½ hours)
5. Do everything possible to be objective and not to lead the group or members. Aim to be objective.

6. Develop the right questions.

A good size for the group is 5-10 people. The interviewees should be as representative as possible of your niche market. Questions should be open-ended, scripted and verbally presented without facilitator bias.

Where else can you go for references, resources, referrals to find your target market or information about them?

Electronic Survey Tools

There are a number of web services that can help you perform your survey. A few of them are: "surveymonkey.com", "polldaddy.com", and 'pollmonkey.com." You will need the respondents email address and permission to send them the questionnaire. Obviously if you have a good amount of email addresses you can obtain a lot of feedback quickly. Keep the questions short and get right to the point. Be careful to not include a preface that might bias their answers. For These three questions will guide you in developing your survey(s). Also remember the "magical" 4W's and H – why, what, when, were and how. These interrogatives are the means to constructing questions.

- Who needs to know what you know?
- What problems can you solve?
- What "pain" can you heal?

Rhetorical questions are not functional. You want a response. You want valid information that hasn't been biased by the questioner or questionnaire

You can ask overhead questions, (to whole group, focused questions, to one particular person or profile, or discounting questions), designed to clarify or discount any assumptions you have.

The most effective four words in finding out what your target market want are: "What do you want?" Every time I meet anyone in healthcare who might remotely need my services or informational products I ask them that question. If they have heard my presentation, I ask them, "What 10 minutes could I take out of the presentation and what could I fill that time with?" This gives me honest and correct feedback on what I could improve. If you audio or video tape the session be sure you obtain permission from the group. The downside of taping is that you have to spend the time reviewing the whole session. The advantages are that you don't need to be taking notes during the session and the tape captures every little nuance of the responses. This is helpful in your tabulation and analysis.

Store the Data

What do you do with the data? Once you have obtained the data for your various surveys you need to analyze the results. Collect each response and organize them into a database. This will allow you to be very precise in the correct interpretation of your markets' needs. You will also be able to refer to this valuable information in the future as you develop new speeches or publications. Although I do not receive compensation for mentioning them, I prefer Microsoft Excel and Access. I am an Access nut. I setup a database for every project and aspect of my life. My colleagues accuse me of having a database of my databases. Just to show you how anal-retentive I am (is there a hyphen in anal-retentive?) I have over 200 books in my library. I have cataloged them in a database with title, author, year printed and topic area. It may seem like I have a lot of time on my hands but as I prepare a new topic, article, or publication, I can quickly go to the database, see what books I have relative to that topic, pull them and save a lot of time not having to rummage through piles and piles of books. I also do this with my paper and electronic files. This saves me an enormous amount of time and allows me to enjoy my favorite activity - going to the movies.

One key principle of data storage is that you store only one piece of data in one field. For example if you collecting information on gender and marriage status separate the two into different fields. If you are collecting street addresses separate the number from the street name. This will allow you to sort and query them with greater accuracy.

Analyze the Data

Stay objective as you analyze the data. This is where you will have an advantage. This is the really exciting part. You will have confirmed that there is a want and need for your particular passion and expertise. This means that there is a great chance your business is going to succeed. It is helpful to have others assist you in the analysis. The more versed they are in your specialty the better. Is the market big enough? You are now ready to address one of the four "P's of marketing -Price. We will discuss product, place and promotion later.

Choose the Best Niche

You are getting there. Remember that candy store; so many opportunities, so many ideas have surfaced from the analysis. This is where it is important to choose where to start. What really is the "core"? What is the heart of your expertise? What will all those other ideas and projects build onto? Write this concise statement out. It should only be one sentence, if that. Print it out in 20 Pt. font. Put it in front or next to your computer. Prioritize and start your strategy – "your strategic plan" on just one market with just one product.

Consider these questions to make sure you have all the data you need:

- Who else is speaking or consulting to my healthcare market(s) with the same content?
- Roughly will my net profit meet my needs?

- Can I maintain the standards and quality of my speaking and consulting outcomes?
- What value will I be providing in healthcare?
- Will I be providing what my healthcare clients actually need?
- How will I remain passionate about my speaking and consulting in healthcare?
- What is the growth potential?

Your Summary Report

You should now have ended up with information from your potential niche clients and audiences regarding:

- how can you meet their needs
- what information and skills do they lack
- what will make them more money
- what will make them more productive

Once you have sifted through all the data you are ready for a conclusion. Create a summary statement such as:

My unique expertise is

_____, and I will

be providing the core topic(s) of

_____

_____,

_____

_____,

of the specific markets of _____,

who have characteristics of _____.

I will provide _____ of speeches at the fee of

$_____ and sell ____ number of Informational

products.

You now are ready to prepare and profit from information that the target market wants (not what you think they should like, think they need, or what you prefer.)

How Will You Be Known?

How do you want to be known? Where do you want to end up in your profession and market?

You are now ready to define your brand. My bias is to brand yourself with your name. You can also have "sub-brands" – catchy phrases

you might create. You can name each of your speeches and informational products with different names, but you will always want to be recognized as you. You might call yourself Joe/Jane Smith.co, "the Critical Care Pro", or Joe/Jane Smith.com, "the Quality Assurance Pro", or Joe/Jane Smith "the Wellness King/Queen." That's ok. Just make sure your name is recognizable and you are seen as the unique expert for your special niche.

What Makes You Unique?

You may have a unique heritage, language, appearance, or personality besides having a unique service or product. You may also have created unique features and benefits in the sales and packaging of your services and products.

Start to Design Your Brand

- Who are you?
- What do you do?
- What is unique about you?
- How do you want the world to know you?
- What image will convey the message that you are going to make your clients and audiences more profitable and productive?

Buy as many domain name versions of your name as you can including the misspellings. Buy those catchy titles that describe your expertise as domain names.

Brand Everything

Put your logo, name, and head shot on everything you produce. Include these branding features on everything you produce. This should include your stationary, business cards, promotional, informational materials, images, and web presence. Have the promoters of the venues where you speak include your image and brand also. Promote everywhere. The average person in the United States receives over 10,000 promotional cues every day. You have to do as much as you can to stand out above the crowd.

Identify Your Unique Value Proposition (UVP)

A UVP is the different and extra value you can give your audiences and clients that nobody else can offer. Other names for UVP are added value and unique selling proposition. What are you especially talented with regarding your personality, philosophy or ability to look at problem situations uniquely? What extra benefits can you deliver that the client or audiences are not expecting. What do you offer customers that your competition does not?

I speak on topics such as tobacco control, preventive medicine and critical care medicine. These topics could be very dry and clinical. I am uniquely able to provide *appropriate* humor that makes my presentation not only informative but entertaining. I have developed this approach over the years because I know others presenting this material don't or cannot. This makes me more marketable and allows me to book much more return presentation with the same clients.

Now is time for you to shine and use that unique creative nature you possess. What will you add to your niche that not only will make you stand out but will be of special value to your audiences and clients?

You must stand out from the crowd. What makes you different from your competitors? What do you offer that appeals to your audiences and clients and will allow them to be more profitable and/or productive? What makes you **unique**? What can you **propose** or offer to your clients or audiences that your competitors are not offering? What can they grasp as a value, something special, or extra?

Some examples of a UVP related to productivity would be providing record keeping and attendance updates for an agency that might send frequent attendees to your programs. You might provide them additional consulting time or sending them current technical information updates. An example of increasing their profit might be discounting your informational products or services, providing referrals of business to them from your contacts, or illustrating to them how your "techniques" will save or gain them money.

In one of my public seminar programs I allow corporations and healthcare agencies to pre-pay at a 30 percent discount to save them many dollars over a year period of time.

Continuously Survey

Look forward, look back. It's all about following the money. What are the trends? What is happening week to week and month to month? What is good and what is bad?

In order to stay up with industry standards and technology you must always be taking the pulse of your niche. All sources and resources should be systematically reviewed.

If you think the material you have developed is perfect, and you keep it that way – it will become stagnant.

I "interview" all healthcare professionals I meet and ask them questions regarding the dreams they have about starting their own business. This input serves as content for future surveys and presentations.

You have to meet the needs of your target market in order to remain competitive and build your practice. Develop a strategic systematic approach that will continuously alert you to the needs of your target market.

The more things change the more they stay the same does not apply to the healthcare and speaking industries. Science and healthcare are continuously evolving monthly. Gone are the days of the overhead projector and straight lecturing to groups. Technology and the science of adult education (Andragogy) have changed since our fathers listened to experts. The new formats of virtual classrooms, chat rooms, digital surveys, and streaming video are now the norm. We must keep up and master these formats if we are going to speak and consult. Technology and your uniqueness will rule.

More than ever our clients and audiences question our statements and demand accountability. Adult learners want to know the why before the how.

This is all good news for us as professional speakers. The process is simple. As we keep our technical expertise science and evidence based, and know exactly what our clients and audiences want, we will continue to succeed. You must set up systems that will guarantee these conditions.

By literally asking every audience and client what they expect or need next, and using research techniques such as Google alerts, and Medsearch, you will be remain ahead of your competition and stay the premier expert in your niche.

Simple questions like "what other informational services do you or your organization need?" can provide you with more material and content then you will ever be able to use.

Google Yourself

Take advantage of "Google Alert." If you sign up for "Google Alerts" (free), they will alert you every time a certain name of term appears on the internet.

I have a Google alert for my name "Dennis Mahoney" – every time my name or any other Dennis Mahoney appears on a search I receive an email. I also have one for some of my clinical areas, - "preventive medicine", and "ACLS", and "cardiopulmonary resuscitation", and "tobacco treatment." The Google alerts will send me new science updates, general industry news and what the competitors are doing. I also have Google alerts regarding my client organizations. This allows me to congratulate them on their accomplishments and gives me a picture on what's going on in their organization that I might be able to provide services for.

Use Pad and Pen

or Digital Voice Recorder (DVR)

Everywhere

In continuously surveying my markets, I keep a pen and pad of paper in every room of my house, my car, and even in my locker at my health club. I have also used a little pocket digital voice recorder to record random thoughts, but now have moved to using a digital voice recorder app on my I-Phone. I make the notes, and then transfer them to the particular document and section that my thoughts or comments relate to. This system of cataloging helps me become better organized, less stressed in finding resources, and eliminates losing the tidbits in piles of papers. I can more easily incorporate that material into my writings, web site, blog, and social media contacts.

Chapter Three

Give them What They Want

How to Price

I am asked all the time, "How much should (or can) I charge for my presentation or informational product?" My regular answer is, "Whatever the market will bear." The problem with that answer is finding out what the market will bear.

It's all about the client and customer. What do they want, not what you want to give them. Success for you comes when the two match.

It is said there are three types of fees: the fee you should receive, the fee you would like to receive, and the fee you get. It is up to you to have them match.

Pricing can be based on several factors: What is the quality of your deliverables, what are they worth in the healthcare industry and how much will the client or audience pay for your services?

Another consideration is the fact that the lower the price the larger the volume, and vice-versa. It really is a personal choice on which one or both plan you implement. Which will you choose? How you position and bundle and offer your services and informational products will drive the model that is successful for you.

"What is your time worth to you?" Although you should never be paid "per hour" for your presentations, your time really is your most valuable asset.

In one of my businesses (profit centers) I sponsor a number of public emergency response certification programs in the metropolitan area where I live. I can deliver a speech or workshop (including travel time) and charge a smaller fee and net more money than someone who travels out of town and spends one to three days traveling and delivering for a higher fee. I consistently gross and net more each and every week, more than most speakers traveling and earning a larger fee. I have also added other services and products with higher fees that allow me to choose when and where I travel. So it really boils down to what you perceive your worth is, when and where you want to speak, and what your market will bear. Considerations for pricing can also include what your competitors are charging, and the economic level within your niche.

Now that you know exactly who needs a specific topic or series of topics or services, you also should have discovered roughly what they will pay under what conditions. How will this fit into your cash flow projections? How will this offset your expenses? Therein lays the goal of being in business – a margin of profit that will meet your needs and expectations.

Years ago it was drummed in to me to make sure I was paid for the "unique worth" and not for "time and materials.

You will find you are being hired by your professional clients and audiences for three reasons – profitability, productivity, and effectiveness. The trick is for you to demonstrate for them the specific gain in their profit, productivity, and effective.

If you consult and setup a process that successfully decreases a healthcare facility's cross contamination and infectious disease rate by 20 percent and that is represented by a $500,000.00 a year savings, what do you think your fee should be? Would $5,000.00, $10,000.00, or even $20,000.00 be high enough?

You need to know what you can deliver in outcomes (deliverables) and even better what additionally can you give them to compete in the marketplace and set your fees appropriately.

What image are you putting forth? This will be reflected in your fee structure.

You are no longer an hourly employee. You are now being paid for your opinion, unique expertise, and technical knowledge and skills.

In another profit center I set my individual registration fee very low. My competitors continuously position their fees at the top of that price range. I continuously price myself at the lowest end of the price range. Given the principle that the lower the price the higher the volume and higher the price the lower the volume, who do you think consistently fills more seats more frequently? This not only gives me higher dollar income but has built up my participant database to over 15,000 attendees. The incremental word of mouth, and return business far outweighs the hit and miss higher fee strategy. This fee fits for this situation. The value to me is being paid to obtain all those email addresses to promote myself further.

In one profit center and niche I speak to there are very few competitors at my level. My fees are high. I position the content it addresses to both productivity and profitability of the audience members.

Philosophically, keep in mind if you're on a mission you don't need a quota.

You must have your monetary needs met along with the adulation to insure you are happy after your presentation.

Try this exercise:

1. Document your expenses for the next year.

2. List all of your business expenses by month for a whole year

3. List your minimum salary and benefits will you need to manage your personal life by month for a whole year

4. List the services and informational products with an assigned price that you will offer to your niche

5. Now calculate how many "units" will have to be sold to meet your business and personal expenses.

This calculation will give you a rough idea of how well you identified the target market that will support your business and the reality of how much volume you can deliver.

Although I love my audiences and love my topics, I found out a long time ago that if I am not compensated for what I feel I am worth and for what I need, and if I don't receive rave reviews from my audiences, then I am very happy.

I insure rave reviews because I effectively conducted my market assessment, prepared well and regardless of the conditions or how I was feeling that day, delivered the most enthusiastic and passionate talk I was capable of delivering. That by the way is the definition of being a professional.

The fee was a result of a process where I concluded what I was worth and promoted myself to the markets that could pay that fee. There are innumerable times when I will speak for various fees and even give no fee speeches. (Never give a free speech – only no fee- we will discuss in those situations are my decision and for a specific strategic reason as opposed to the market dictating my fees.

So boost your self-confidence and self-image, do your "speaking due diligence" and stick to a fee structure that will meet your needs.

Formalize and Formulate Your Unique Expertise

So far you have: 1) confirmed your passion, 2) prioritized your expertise, 3) identified your market and their ability to pay you, 4) decided on your niche, and 5) designed your brand.

It's time to "formalize" your expert knowledge and skills by putting it in a form, structure or flow. You will now transfer your knowledge from your head into a concrete format. You need to document it in forms that your clients and audiences can benefit from through your expertise.

You have chosen a niche market, analyzed it and now know they want and need your expertise. They are waiting for you and want you. You are enthused about your message and the audience.

Only spend time and your energy on content that can be transformed into promotion or sales of your informational products and services.

Your service or product must be saleable. You have to prepare your information for sale, because you are in the information selling business.

This is where a large percentage of people fail. They stick to the previous safe "surveying stage." They don't move to action steps and develop their services and products (remember the "fear of success" factor.) Don't get caught in this trap. This is payoff time. After you finish this section you are ready to start earning money the next day. You will have something to sell.

Solve a Problem, Heal the Pain

Who needs to know what you know? What problems can you solve, what "pain" can you heal? Meet these needs and wants:

1. Common personal issues (illness, hunger, thirst, danger)
2. Comfort issues (pain, injury)
3. Emotional issues (grief, hurt, fear, anger, sorrow, confusion, embarrassment, tension, worry)
4. Being successful
5. Making and saving money
6. Be recognized
7. Saving time
8. To belong
9. Being productive
10. Being profitable

Interview healthcare executives, practitioners, vendors, patients and clients for their problem stories

What will your clients and audiences need when they leave you? What will they need over the next week, month, or year? Build these needs into your all your deliverables. Design your "system" with these considerations.

Content is King

You are an expert. The niche you have chosen is unique and special. The message and format in which you deliver your information has to meet the highest standards. The development and delivery is critical towards building your speaking and consulting practice. Quality is number one for you to maintain valid up to date information in an assessable format. If you strive for quality, then you will be successful. Exceptional delivery and added value will put you and keep you on top.

The goal is to be innovative. Come up with something new and/or unique and progressive.

Your business only grows if you deliver value and quality – over and over!

Sell the Outcome and Give it All Away

Share all your expertise with your audiences and clients. The more information you give up, the more you will be motivated to research and develop more for your expertise. This approach will take you to a higher level. Deliver what the client or audience member will need not what you are all about. Focus on the benefits of your expertise.

Although they are paying you for your uniqueness, they want your knowledge. We persuade, entertain, and inform and the clients and audiences pay us to transfer our skills, systems and processes to them. They want to be more productive. The ideal transfer quickly changes their behavior permanently towards those ends.

You Can't Get Paid If You Aren't Offering Something

I ask my clients all the time "what do you have scheduled for a speech or what product have you finished?" They respond, "Oh nothing, I can't get my fee." or "I am still writing some new material." or "I am not sure what the audience wants."

It really doesn't matter why you are not making money. You can't stay in business and do the thing that you are good at and love unless you make money.

To be successful you have to make and measure a difference for your client and audience.

Saleable Information Purposes

▪ Help them produce more profits
▪ Help them become more productive
▪ Update them to current standards
▪ Help them promote their services
▪ Help them become more efficient
▪ Help them become more effective
▪ Help them become more productive
▪ Help them manage better
▪ Help them communicate better

Potential Replication (leveraging) Opportunities

▪ Information in a systematic format (a system)
▪ Design a "process"
▪ In-person one on one coaching/consulting
▪ In-person group – lectures, keynotes, seminars, boot camps, workshops
▪ One-on-one telephone
▪ Tele-conferences, Webinars, virtual classrooms
▪ Print – Book, tips-booklet, Manuals, white papers
▪ Media – CD's, DVD's, MP3, e-books, PDF files, Podcasts, videos

Where Do You Start

The saying "Which came first the chicken or the egg?" rears its ugly head here. Do you write a book first and then "replicate or leverage" the pieces of the book into speeches, small print, and electronic formats, or do you develop short smaller focused pieces of information and combine them all into a book or speech. The good news is you can do whichever you prefer and makes the most sense to you in supporting your business model and strategic plan.

Whichever process you choose, you must start with valid and current guidance from your market assessment. To overlook this step or not listen to the results would be foolish. Your exact market analysis and special expertise will make you a winner.

Replicate, Replicate

The most effective strategy of increasing revenue from your expertise or intellectual property is to provide information in other formats. This is called re-purposing or leveraging.

Someone once said "If you are going to tell it, then sell it." Without informational products you are only as financially stable as your last speech. You need to replicate every word you say (and think). You can now leverage or maximize those spoken words into many more formats and sell that same message to additional audiences and clients. So where do you start? What exactly do you write? How long should your documents be? In this two trillion dollar industry someone is looking for your expertise and they may want it in many formats.

Document or record every speech. Leverage or maximize your information in as many formats as possible, such as a books, manuals, tips booklets, quick reference cards, audio or video recordings, or web based electronic books and recordings. You can also replicate yourself by hiring instructors or speakers to deliver your information or you can license various parties to distribute and present your content. You might join in a partnership or affiliate with one or more parties to promote your content.

If you say it, then also write it and record it. So go out speak in the town square, go to local business groups, church groups, radio shows, cable TV, and do anything but do something. This is a good time and chance to hone your material and record the speeches. It also will bring you more and more bookings and money. Publicity will come proportionally.

Replication occurs by documenting all your expertise in some communicative permanent form. In today's world those forms are in print, digital audio and/or video formats. The most effective model for your speaking practice to thrive is to replicate every word and thought of your expertise that you possess in your brain.

The great benefit of being a unique content expert is you only have to develop your material once. As a speaker/writer/consultant you can format or leverage that same information and be receiving revenue from the information from many different formats, without presenting it in person.

Get Organized

Before you embark upon any task for your business first say to yourself "Who can do this for me?" In reality there are very few tasks that can't be farmed out. Employ others to research, edit, copy, or explore the publication options. Be that good manager and writer. If you love to speak but do not like to write then you will need to delegate. Remember the definition of a good manager is "one who delegates." Manage your practice well.

If you love to speak, know your area of expertise well, but don't like to spend the time writing, then be that good manger and delegate the writing to others. You can find writers at your local university – either the faculty or graduate students. You can search Craig's List, or Elance.com, and any number of other referral services on the internet. Generally you will propose the work that needs to be written and applicants will bid on your job. They will submit references and credentials. Their fees are very reasonable.

Do all the internet and web services and features scare you? Do these electronic gadgets stress you out? Are you not into gadgets? (I, myself have never met a three prong plug or USB connection I didn't like.) If you are not, however, then consider the many internet services that you can hire to do your transcription, editing and production of your audio/video products. These formats can be duplicated for distribution or be available as downloadable speeches and publications from your web sites.

You also have available digital voice recorders and voice recognition programs that will record your content and store it in digital format on your computer. In addition, there are individuals available through the above internet services who will transcribe your audio files into print format for as little as one cent per word. Programs such as Audacity, Soundforge, Camtasia, and Pinnacle allow you to record, edit, and produce audio, video, power point and combinations of the three rights in your own office.

Get Rid Of Writers Block

I don't know if there is really such a thing as writer's block. I do know there are things such a TV, cleaning out the closet, playing or taking the dog for a walk, etc. that are the culprits which stop us from finishing whatever we are writing. You need to protect your motivation, passion, and protect our "author time" and not let life get in the way.

There will always be something, especially those little distractions that will sabotage you.

When you start a writing project try to finish it as fast as you can. To drag it on over an extended period of time can lessen your love of the topic and project.

Don't Multi-Task

Do not multitask when you develop your content even if you are writing in 30 minutes sessions. Keep them uninterrupted. You will produce more succinct, focused content if you can maintain a "laser focus" on your message.

One Document at a Time

If there is only one piece of advice I could offer you in writing any one article or manuscript it is to work on only one word document for each. Name that document as specific as you can and add the date you started in the title, as part of the name. It is not a good idea to also start a folder for the group of similar writings in one given project.

Work on one project at a time to be effective. It is unrealistic to divide your mental acuity and energy on more than one project and produce quality. It's all about focus and clarity. Having said that, you can however, write in "snippets'. Compose a paragraph at a time or skip around as you write. Don't think of the book as one long thought process that you have to start and finish as a whole document. That will overwhelm you.

Finish each project before you start to edit. If you try to edit your past work at the beginning of each new session you will never finish the project.

Wrote is Better Then Right

As Nike says, "Just do it." Eat that elephant one thought at a time (on paper). Your writing will never be perfect in your eyes. You can spin your wheels and spend years "perfecting" your works. Start putting everything in your head on paper. Get it out of there. Editors will prepare the final version. Have fun now getting started. Starting is 90 percent of finishing the job.

Writing That Book

A book is defined as a written literary work. We know formats today can not only be written but also produced in either digital audio or video formats. With the advent of podcasts, apps, Kindle, electronic readers, and other electronic mediums there are numerous ways we can develop and buy books.

Your book(s) doesn't have to include everything in the world in its first edition. Your blogs, web site, white papers, tips booklets, and presentations can serve as additional outlets serving your audiences

and clients. There will always be a never ending project to try to include everything. Remember "wrote is better than right." You will get a chance to add your body of work through many of those other formats and venues.

There are a number of approaches to organizing and writing your Pulitzer Prize. Over the years I have written hundreds of presentations, workshops, seminars, clinical and technical manuals, protocols, policies and procedural publications. I can put the "expertise" to paper. I have written over one million dollars' worth of grants and RFP's. I did not receive A's in English writing classes in school, so I need an editor to deal with grammatical and structure correctness. That is why I hire the best editor I can find. An editor can work with your prose, grammar and page layout. Unless you have a strong professional background in editing, an editor probably is more efficient and skilled at sculpturing your content into that masterpiece you envision.

It is a lot easier for the editing and publishing efforts if you decide

what size your book will be before you start writing so you can set your margins accordingly.

A book gives you credibility as an author, gathering your body of knowledge on one particular area of expertise, and serving as a foundation for leveraging your intellectual properties. Depending on your conditions and needs, techniques on developing your project can vary.

If you have conducted an effective market analysis, start with a book and then use the content for the basis of other formats. The process of finishing the book can be relatively simple.

By identifying your brief description, and bulleted features and benefits of the content you have really also written your core outline.

The parts of a book:

The book layout can contain:

1. Front cover
2. Inside cover
3. Title page
4. Copyright page
5. Acknowledgements
6. Foreword
7. Preface
8. Introduction
9. Table of contents
10. Chapter page
11. Chapter content -   anecdotes, stories, case studies, lists, images, suggestions, assignments
12. References
13. Business promotions

14. Inside back cover
15. Back cover- As Dan Poynter, the expert in writing books suggests, start with the back cover. This is what the buyer will look at first. The back cover should include:
    o Descriptive sub title of your book
    o Short description of the direction and scope of the content
    o Some biographical description of yourself
    o Bulleted benefits of the content of the book
    o Publisher name
    o Price
    o ISBN number and bar code

It seems every book has a preface and introduction. You can do anything you want with the text in these sections. I have used the preface to outline the benefits and features of the content of this book, and the introduction to set the tone and process. In your writing, determine which questions you are answering for your reader. Is it "How", and/or "Why", and/or "What."

At a later date you will more than likely come out with a second edition. Prepare a document for "add-ons." Arrange the document with your chapter headings and daily or weekly enter your new information under these headings. It will be much easier to edit the second edition using this method.

Always Tell a Story

Recently the longtime producer of the TV show "60 Minutes", Don Hewitt, passed away. He was credited with his almost 30 years of successful episodes because he had one clear criterion for his interviewers and editors: "Tell me a story."

We all like stories. The best speakers and writers are the ones who tell a story. I continuously gather case studies and anecdotes of my clients and professional experiences. They help me in my speeches and publications to emphasize a key point.

It's all about focus and clarity. You must set a linear path in developing your content in order to accomplish each piece of a project.

Don't get lost in process steps – stay focused on content.

Develop something every day. Try not to block out more than two to three hours a day for writing.

Whether you are writing an article for a professional journal or writing an entire book, you want to be time and energy efficient.

We all have that folder of ideas and projects to do. How many of those ever get started, much less finished? It is said that 80 percent of what we put into a file (paper or electronic) never gets seen again. Is this just another passive avoidance mechanism by filling this file up with dozens of ideas? It's ok to have that file but don't spend your time filling the file – spend the time doing the file, one project at a time.

Write out a statement describing the end point of your current project. Put a deadline to it. Put time allotment to each sub task. Commit to the schedule and finish it. Do all this before you start another speech or topic? Decide the scope and steps of your project. Identify and list the process steps, resources, anticipated obstacles and outcomes. This approach will save time and bring you a fee sooner.

It's all about them. Content should reflect their needs. It is said that if you write or speak really well your audience members will tell thirty other people, if you do poorly they will tell fifty people

For the sake of simplification and discussion let's use the "book" format as our writing example. You will be using this content for your presentations.

What process and content development steps would you need to follow to finish the book and eventually lead to your presentations and other works?

Remember when you finish the book you have a wealth of text to transform or leverage into many other forms of information for your clients and audiences.

Include statistics and facts in your text and presentations. People like points of reference and the extra added tidbits serve to keep the audience or reader interested.

There are also many ways to approach your writing, but as you address each topic in your book consider including a definition, description, purpose, benefits, features, and uses. Ask yourself: what would the reader like to know? (Answer the questions what, where, why, when and how). In general a book should explain what and why. Manuals, workshops, book camps, learning systems etc.., are to explain how.

If you are going to write there are a few methods that work for me. I have included the processes that have worked for me for over 25 years. I have updated the process as technology and science has evolved and continues to add my personal input to all the content. These processes will save you 80 percent of your usual development time and guarantee that you deliver exactly what was expected by your client or audience with 100 percent accuracy.

General Techniques

Based on your research findings, a general approach is to identify your main point and highlights of your topic, and visualize your readers as "students." What would be all the questions you would ask them and want them to answer correctly and demonstrate that they know your material perfectly? What questions would they ask? These questions will be the chapter headings, paragraph headings, etc… for your publication. Write them out, sort them into categories, list them and then answer them individually and randomly. Your publication is finished.

Technique One: "Drain your Brain"

This method allows you to include every little morsel of information you want to include in the document, and will save you the most amount of time in finishing the project.

Step 1) Open up a blank document.

Step 2) Save the document with the date, general category, and specific topic name.

Step 3) Identify 5 – 10 major categories within your topic area. For example if your topic was "How to interpret an EKG", your categories might be anatomy, cardio-physiology, EKG patterns, machines, and patients. The first letter of those five categories are A, C, E, M, and P.

Step 4) daily or weekly, randomly think of any "snippets", and enter them into your document. Try to make each entry no more than a sentence in length.

Step 5) as you enter each entry, type the category letter in front of the entry. The entry can be typed with the category letter to the left of your document. As you continue to add entries the documents will grow.

Step 6) at a point in time, when you determine that you have a substantial volume of text, you can choose "select all" on your tool bar. Once all text is highlighted, you can now choose the "a-z" sort function on your toolbar, and then choose "sort by paragraph and text." Every sentence in your document will be sorted by the first letter of the sentence and consequently by category. These categories are now your main sections or chapters of your book.

Technique Two: "Two Way Interviewing"

Given that you have gathered your primary and secondary market survey sources, you can now question or interview a select few of those sources for more specific content for your topic.

Step 1) Using open ended questions, ask "Why, What, and How" questions of each main category of your main headings and sub points in your topic area. Interview your sources with questions, such as: "Why do you need to learn how to implement the seven steps of primary prevention? What would you do with the techniques, and how would you implement those steps in your medical practice?

Step 2) if you allow each respondent to talk long enough, they will provide you with deep and focused content that will add tremendously to your document outline.

Step 3) you might even ask for quotes from the respondents that you can not only include in the text but also use for testimonials in your promotion.

You can also reverse this technique and have them interview you. Record the session. As you play it back you will be amazed at the amount of information you had given out that you normally wouldn't

have thought about. (Remember you are a speaker – you love to talk!).

Technique Three: "In Their Shoes"

Step 1) you can also take on that third person role and imagine from your experiences and/or with the experiences of your colleagues what the key questions, needs, and activities are included in the professional lives of your clients and audiences. For example If you are providing information to new physical therapists on building their private practice, you might know from experience that they need to understand the basic tenets of writing non-complete contracts for their employees.

Step 2) you will then include this as a sub category under "Legal Concerns.", Step 3) you are able now to research and expand this sub-topic, thus adding more valuable content to the reader or audiences.

Technique Four: "Unique Value Proposition"

Step 1) either build or obtain an email list of prospective respondents that you would like to consider attending a no fee lecture, workshop or teleconference on a particular topic.

Step 2) Mail out a request for them to respond back to you with just their name, email address, and answer this one question, "What would you like to receive as an extra added value from my presentation or informational product?"

Step 3) Once you have received a fair number of responses back, you now have very focused questions that will not only guide your content development for that no fee session, but give you an extensive list of benefits that will move you head and shoulders above your competition.

Step 4) because these responses are the main choices of the respondents, the information you deliver from this input will be always be a cut above the basic knowledge they need to know. This fact is the definition of "unique value proposition." It is the special thing that sets you apart from your competitors in the market.

Chapter Four

Become a
Speaking Star

Love your message, love your audience

There are two great considerations in formatting your presentations:

1) "There are always three presentations: the one you plan, the one you give, and the one you wish you gave."

2) "Tell them what you're going to tell them, tell them, and then tell them what you told them."

Good advice to guide your presentations.

Whether it is a speech, book, blog, or other format you are communicating, you will either be persuading, entertaining, educating or a combination of the three.

Now that you have a large amount of your expertise centralized in a book, you are ready to use portions of the content in many formats. Let's start with a review of the application of that content for live speaking formats.

Important Speaking Considerations

To stay competitive and remain habitual:

- Be confident, fired up, passionate, and keep your energy high
- Always show up and be on time
- Maintain the highest level of professionalism.
- Never cancel or postpone a presentation.
- Evaluate your past presentation with the question - Would you hire yourself back?
- Make each presentation as if it was your last one: high quality and high energy

Murphy's Law will take care of enough problems and issues popping up. In twenty five years plus, I have given over 4000 presentations. I have never been late for any presentations and only had to reschedule two or three because of extreme family and personal situations.

There have been many occasions that I didn't want to speak or that it was personally inconvenient. I am a professional, that was all there was to it. The least desirable the audience or circumstances the more I have learned to psyche myself up to do the same level of presentation I would deliver in the best of circumstances. With these habits you develop discipline and the highest level of professionalism by delivering consistent quality every time.

Sell Yourself – All the Way Through

Although your audiences and clients want your information, they also want a unique, even controversial opinion that you might possess.

You will become successful if you remain true to yourself. Along with your technical expertise, your audiences and clients want your unique perspective. They want your opinions, complaints, philosophical views, your different persona, and special connection you have established with them.

How can you be innovative by going against the norm, or the common wisdom? What different problem solving approach can be fresh and successful for your clients and audiences?

The ones who don't value you will not be your clients. That is ok. It's a big world out there and you are not going to please all people. You don't want to. There are some people out there that you will be thankful don't come.

You must learn to be an unapologetic self-promoter. You might have the best information in the world and deliver it eloquently but if nobody hears or reads it it's all for naught.

Identify Your Signature Story

My audiences remember me not only from skills and outcomes they retained after our involvements, but also a signature story that accompanied that involvement. My basic and advanced cardiovascular care courses for first responders and critical care personnel include a couple stories of my resuscitation efforts outside of the hospital setting with neighbors or close relatives. My tobacco treatment medical provider workshops include stories of the client counseling sessions and managing patients dying from lung and breathing crisis as a result of smoking cigarettes. My own story of starting my speaking business includes my signature of quitting my full time job two weeks after listening to the authors of *What Color Is My Parachute* (Crystal and Boles) on the Tom Snyder TV show. That night, that show changed my life.

Make your stories full of impact. As a male, I shop for clothes rarely. Fortunately my wife is the expert clothes shopper in the family. When I do shop, it always amazes me that when I see something in the store it seems to be more striking than when I wear it in public. Our stories are the same way. We really have to put a lot of color and fashion in our stories to have an impact on people.

Here Are the Top Seven Secrets of Being a Star

1. You must always plan or "script" your presentations from hello to goodbye.
2. Never make your first rehearsal in front of your audience. Rehearse the presentation 4-5 times minimum.
3. Operate from a checklist.
4. Have all contact information (including cell phone) from your sponsor.
5. Arrive one hour early (local); one day earlier (distance)
6. Think FUN! Your attitude and behavior will be mirrored by the audience or client.

7. Leave your personal problems behind you – your audience and clients can be an oasis and safe ground for you.

Presentation Skills Basics

Verbal – word choices – carefully incorporate jargon, scientific terminology and acronyms into your content that is relative to the background and level of the audience.

There is nothing more embarrassing than for you to mispronounce a medical term to a group of professionals. Know your audience and their specialty areas well. In today's expanding worldwide marketplace we must be culturally competent and culturally sensitive to our audiences. I speak to a large number of community healthcare agencies in my city. These groups represent thirty seven languages and many more countries of origin. I really do have to know my audiences before I present or consult.

Vocal- (the sound of your voice) - volume, pitch, pauses, quality, inflection, rate, emphasis, are all tools to use to accomplish longer retention of your message for your audiences.

Non-Verbal (what the audiences see) – gestures, eye contact, body movement. All three of these components should be measured, rehearsed, natural, and designed not to distract the audience, but support and accentuate your message.

A Quick Lesson Regarding Humor

Only five percent of speakers can use humor naturally, the other 95 percent can use it if they learn the skills and rehearse. It's hard work. Years ago my wife gave me a gift certificate to a stand-up comedy school in New York City. She said, "You're not funny – so go learn how to be." I actually got my first chance to do stand-up in a major New York comedy club. I only had five minutes. It took me over four days and about twenty five rehearsals to develop those five minutes. (I had them rolling in aisles by the way.)

There is a science to using humor and that's a whole other book. Educate yourself if you are going to use humor in your presentations and writings.

The Best Presentation Notes

Don't use index cards. I have seen speakers drop their pile of index cards and spend the next few minutes picking up and re-arranging the cards in order again. – use a series of numbered text boxes on numbered sheets of paper in 18 pt. font.

If it is appropriate, I love to use power point slides in the most effective way possible. No "death by power point' for me or my audiences.   There are my notes right up on the screen. I can use images, video clips, graphics, and cartoons to emphasize my main points.

```
POINT S

    .....................

    .....................
```

Sure Fire Guide to Outcome Based Speaking

There is a large trend moving away from keynote speeches. The National Speaking Association (NSA), the premier national organization of professionals who make their living speaking, reports that over 70 percent of their member's businesses are involved in training or outcome based education. More and more organizations and associations are looking for fast, current, and practical techniques on how to be more profitable and productive. Workshops, seminars, tele-conferences, and webinars are the wave of the future. Live and Video formats will rule the day. Today audiences expect to communicate with the speaker, have their questions answered and be delivered outcome based content.

Bloom's Taxonomy and Domains of Learning

Benjamin Bloom, an educational psychologist, developed a system called the operationalization of educational objectives. His work primarily was with adults and emphasized that adults need to know the "why" before the "how." Your audience absorbs your presentations and expertise in three domains (ways): cognitive, psycho-motor, and affective.

A. The cognitive domain is the total absorption by your audience of the content, purpose, and concepts of your topic.
B. The psycho-motor domain deals with the retention of a mechanical skill (i.e. speaking, storytelling, humor) through repetition.
C. The affective domain is developing a supportive attitude and concern for the topic you are delivering.

Chapter Five

How to
Be Everywhere

Use All the Tenets of Andragogy

Andragogy is defined as the science of adult learning. Use of the principles of Andragogy increases your effectiveness in your presentations with your audiences.

Malcolm Knowles, the father of Andragogy, highlighted four basic tenets of Andragogy:

1. The need to know — adult learners need to know why they need to learn something before undertaking to learn it. Learner self-concept — adults need to be responsible for their own decisions and to be treated as capable of self-direction.
2. Role of learners' experience —adult learners have a variety of experiences of life which represent the richest resource for learning. These experiences are however imbued with bias and presupposition.
3. Readiness to learn —adults are ready to learn those things they need to know in order to cope effectively with life situations.
4. Orientation to learning —adults are motivated to learn to the extent that they perceive that it will help them perform tasks they confront in their life situations.

Some additional principles of Andragogy:

How well do you do in weaving the principles of Andragogy in your presentations. Score yourself from 1-10, 1 being the lowest, 10 being the highest.

YOUR SCORE	ANDRAGOGY TENETS
	You eliminate all barriers to transferring your knowledge and skills to the audience
	You acknowledge the audience is always right
	You assess and prepare the audience is ready to learn
	Your information is valuable and worthwhile
	Your information is problem centered to people (not just facts)
	You incorporate a mechanism for the audience to be self-directed – learner capable, competent, independent
	Your information is related to the audiences' life experiences
	You provide "word" efficiency
	You provide interaction
	You provide empathy
	You give absolute respect
	You endear your audience
	You facilitate as well as present
	You provide for diverse cultural and learning styles
	You incorporate and measure motivation in your presentation
	You identify barriers early
	You guide without directing
	You pre and post assess your whole program strategies and components
TOTAL =	

How did you score!

180 to 151 - You are a speaking star
150 to 100 - You have good instincts
99   to   51 - Your audiences are looking for more
0   to   50 - The good news- there is no way to go but up

Adults like to see the big picture. In my presentations I explain the "what", then the "why", and then the "how."

A good learning objective or goal statement should contain:

1. Measurable outcomes
2. Timeline
3. Goal that can be controlled
4. Action plan with small steps
5. Accountability

You must develop your speeches and books into many formats in order to sustain your business. By offering your intellectual property in many formats you are "leveraging' that information that will appeal to many sub-segments of your niche market. There are a number of live formats you can use to communicate your expertise.

One to Two Hour Keynote

Keynote Speaker – the goal of a keynote speech is to provide impact and sustainability. If you leave your audiences with a "wow" message and they remember and even apply that message over a long period you have done your job.

The keynote speaker traditionally presents to the entire conference or convention registrants. The role of a key note speaker can be to initiate or end a meeting and deliver a "theme" message for the entire meeting, deliver news breaking announcements, or serve to motivate the group in their mission. A key note generally is delivered anywhere from 1-2 hours to 100 – 10,000 attendees. The content usually is built around 1-4 key points per hour. You can obtain very specific details from your main contact of the group you are speaking to, and include anecdotes, personal stories and references or recent activities of the group in your content. Remember if you are going to use humor rehearse thoroughly before you present to the audience. The best style for delivering a keynote is your own style. Be true to yourself; trust in yourself, you have the best persona for delivering your message.

I have delivered key note speeches on preventive medicine to healthcare practitioners over the last fifteen years. My "take home" obviously is preventing disease. This could be a very dry and redundant talk for the audience who spend their careers working exactly towards this end. I am able to make the presentation more interesting by introducing facts such as, only 5per cent of all healthcare dollars in spent on prevention as opposed to the 95per cent of dollars spent on treating the disease after it occurs. I ask them if they know what Willie Sutton, the bank robber said when he was asked why he robbed banks. His answer was, "That's where the money is." Ninety Five percent of money is spent on treating disease because that is where the healthcare system pays the most. I also include a very simple and applicable model called the "prevention model" and show the practitioners how they can develop not only effective and real prevention programs, but profit centers for their agencies. I accomplish my goal of meeting their needs by appropriately and effectively including humor, energy, and a practical application that will add to their profit and productivity in their jobs.

One Hour Breakout

Breakout sessions usually consist of anywhere from one to four presenters within 45 – 60 minutes. Attendees choose this session from a number of other sessions scheduled at the same time. The size of the group can range from a few to over one hundred attendees. The topics are very narrow and are 85per cent presentation with 15per cent of their time allotted for questions from the audience. The content is usually technical applications and processes. The "panel of experts" allows for varied opinions and sharing of more unique outlooks on a topic. The one speaker format gives the audience a more linear and specific approach to the content. You can speak without audio-visual support or use the tried and true power point presentation. We will cover a number of helpful hints on managing your session later in this chapter.

Some speakers function as trainers. They can lead a breakout session at a conference, in-house training, or sponsor their own public workshops. These sessions usually consist of anywhere from 60 minutes to a whole week. Generally the content addresses technical skills, interpersonal and communication skills, or leadership and management techniques. Sometimes certificates of completion and even continuing education units are awarded at the end of the session.

One Half to One Day Seminar or Workshop

Seminars are designed to allow for more of a fifty per cent presentation – fifty per cent attendee interaction. The format can range anywhere from one – three hour sessions, to many full day sessions. The purpose can be to delve deeper into higher level concepts or skills. The learning process should be evaluated in level of knowledge retained, the change in attitude and proficiency in the new knowledge and/or skill.

Your content should:

- Be narrow and focused
- Provide benefit
- Provide skill
- Be descriptive

One of my training businesses involved sponsoring one – two day workshops every week, in five major cities in the United States. That's when flying was fun. (Kind of explains why I really choose when and where I travel nowadays). The two days were six hours of content each day and generally had one focus relating to critical and emergency care. Our market was critical care personnel. We focused our market, assessed correctly and organized ourselves very efficiently. The format for the day started with theory, latest evidence based research, and moved to more skill building discussions, demonstrations and practice. This is the format the clinicians asked for. We followed good Andragogy guidelines and teaching evidence based techniques.

In developing and presenting hundreds of workshops and seminars, I have learned one thing always over prepare and think you are not giving enough, or that the audience will move as fast with the material as you present. It is often not the case. Remember you are the expert. They are there to increase their learning curve during your session.

These are my 10 steps to meeting the needs of the audience:

- Focus on your passion and expertise for this topic
- Confirm audience interest (market assessment)
- Update science based content research
- Define outcome
- Develop outcome measurements
- Develop speech outline and logistics
- Design any supportive media or materials

- Customize group dynamics plan
- Build in "Tenets of Andragogy"
- Review presentation skills
- If demonstrating a skill – make it correct the first time
- Include anecdotes stories, "case studies", and stories of failure

Tele-Conference – Beyond the Speech

Technology has made telephone conference calls an easy and very common format to communicate with large groups. You can arrange for a tele-conference company such as Freeconferencecall.com. or GoToMeeting.com. to coordinate a multi-telephone line informational session. You are given a phone number, and access code for yourself and the participants receive the same phone number but a slightly different access code. You may schedule your session anytime for any length of time within a given period of time. The cost is free and services will record, and transcribe the sessions for a fee. Generally the session lasts for up to one hour.

After the session, the recordings can be turned into CD's, print publications or electronic audio and print files. These informational products can then be sold or given away as additional offerings. You can provide these sessions as a onetime session, or part of a series. The tele-conference can be for a fee or for no fee, depending on your strategic purpose(s). Audoacrobat.com will also provide recording options.

Webinar

If you combine power point, video and tele-conference format you have a webinar virtual classroom. This model combines the webinar, live survey, and chat room formats to come very close to that ideal interactive presenting venue. You may sponsor a single or multiple series of sessions. These sessions can be recorded and made available for purchase or free down-loadable .

Video Conference

Video conferencing is an approach that you can communicate with your client both with audio and video in real time. Today with inexpensive video cameras that attach to your computer you can present yourself with or without power point slides. It can be interactive with the client and allow for questions and answers. It can also be recorded and saved to your archives. You can explain and show complex skills or techniques to all on the call. This method saves the client from traveling and can be offered at more flexible times of the day or evening. There are a number of companies that will arrange the call, record and register participants for the call.

Bootcamp

An informational Boot Camp is usually one or more days when participants are involved in an intensive, focused, and structured process to learn how to accomplish a specific set of skills. Each Boot Camp session should only last as long as the participant can tolerate the learning process. If the agenda and curriculum is too intensive the participant will not meet your desired learning outcome.

The advantage of the breakout sessions, seminar, boot camp, tele-conference, webinar and podcasts over the keynote is that it allows you to deliver more information thus building your business and netting more income.

Coaching

Some of your audience members and clients will request individual and customized assistance in solving their problems. The in vogue term for this in business these days is coaching. I will share with you the benefits, skills and strategies of coaching further in the book under the Consulting section.

Develop Print and Web based Informational Products

If you have thought it, written it, or spoken it, then put it on your web site. You can put it there for no fee or for a fee. Every little thought, opinion, theory, or manuscript should be on your web sites. Get it all out of your head. Replicate your live spoken word and publications to maximize income. Digital format is the current trend and wave of the future. Today there is a multitude of software and technical experts who can assist you in developing your digital audio or video formats. Get help.

If you have delivered a speech, then you are seventy five percent of the way finished with producing your first audio product. Most laptops come equipped with a built in microphone. You can purchase an advanced microphone and pre-amp to use with your computer for a total of $200.00. There is free software to record or edit your informational products (Audacity can be downloaded for free) or software for purchase such as Soundforge by Sony.

You simply prepare your script, bring up your software, hit record, and off you go. You can record any length you would like. You can choose the considerations for the length are size and storage of the file. There are various formats that files can be saved as. I suggest your audios don't last any longer than 40 minutes. You know what they say about participants in our audience, "The mind can absorb what the rear can endure." It's the same for our recordings. How long can you sit and listen to a recording?

Another rationale for a 40 minute length is that it is an average amount of time people commute. This is a great time for your client to listen to your focused concepts.

With digital cameras and flip video informational products that include a USB connection, you can upload video interviews and other content to your web site, YouTube, and I-Tunes in minutes.

Technical specialists will take your audio or video material and edit them. They can add, delete or generally "clean up" your audio material or add background scenes, music or sound effects to your videos. You can use a webcam, simple video camera, flip video camera and/or Camtasia to prepare your video for your editor.

The digital and electronic formats include:

- CD
- DVD
- MP3
- Portable document format (PDF)
- Podcast
- Online videos
- Embedded in other web sites
- Phone apps
- Combinations of all the above

Book

Earlier we discussed the book format. This content can now be "re-purposed" into many print and electronic formats.

Tips Booklets

This publication usually includes quick reference guides that assist you to learn or implement a new process or skill. They can be printed as a deck of cards, laminated sheet, small booklet (can fit in a #10 envelope), or any other format that will be effective to appeal to your clients. They can range anywhere from 1- 100 "tip" statements.

Construct each tip with the tip statements containing one sentence with an action verb, a second sentence with the "how to" implement the action verb, and a third sentence to describe why you are implementing the action verb. You could include more action verbs in the sentence but this might confuse the reader. The supportive sentences are directive and provide clarity. The tips can be categorized into sections. Print the publication in 14 pt. font. Include a coupon for other informational services and informational products in all.

Tips Sheet

A tips sheet can be an 8 ½ x 11 sheet (plastic bound or not), or post card size, or even business card size. You could construct the format as the "classic" tip with the three sentences, or you could list the "steps of ...." as a "system" on the sheet. Some speakers use a post card size format with their book cover on the front and the benefits and features of the book along with a tear off section for the potential client on the back.

Manual

For interest and effective learning you can extend beyond the book to a self-paced process including exercises, interactive scenarios, anecdotes, "to do" assignments", graphs, cartoons, quotes, forms, and other resources. The manual can be tied into a teleconference, webinar, bootcamp, or more extended presentations.

One set of two manuals I have written issues of tobacco treatment and tobacco control. The tobacco treatment manual is designed for healthcare and social services professionals to assess and treat the nicotine dependent patient. The first manual contains the latest science based guidelines, counseling principles, and relapse prevention skills, including actual case studies taken for the hundreds of clients and patients I have counseled. I added my sample forms, assessment tools, and extensive print and web based resources available for the reader. I also include my contact information in the event that if they buy the manual before hearing me speak, they might want to hire me to conduct a keynote or workshop regarding my process.

E-Books

Any publication you have written can be hosted on the web. Generally the publication is in a Portable Document File (PDF) format that does not allow the reader or buyer to change the content and format. You can host the publication on your web site, others sites, or as a separate web site. You can offer it for a fee or free. You can also re-purpose the publication into free or for fee white papers, tips booklets, or sheets, manuals, or 'systems.

Systems and Home Study Programs

Develop a system. Your audience and clients will need a comprehensive and complete process to achieve their goals. Your system will be a compilation of all your recommendations and information in a logical and understandable format.

Your system to your clients and audiences might only be one book, or one manual, or a five inch binder with twelve CD's and and/or DVDs. The size will be driven by the amount and level of information required.

You also might divide your information into levels or specific topics within your niche. This is the magic of professionals speaking. The choices are all up to you and your expertise of the topic and industry you are serving.

More than likely your clients would like to learn everything you know about their and your niche. If you arrange everything you know in a well-organized fashion – you have developed a "system." Pretty basic yes, a "system" has two features – it is designed to accomplish a measurable outcome. This outcome usually will be a permanent change in behavior (the definition of learning) and it is layered in a linear systematic flow that supports the steps of Andragogy (the study of adult learning). This system can also be delivered in person in parts or its entirety.

Membership Site

Consider the above twenty two methods of delivering your content, and imagine arranging them into various packages. You can offer various packages to your clients and audiences under a membership structure. For example you might offer each format separately at one price, or one tele-conference a month for a year and a boot camp as a separate package, or one two minute podcast and your book in another package. One level might be called the "Gold", while another is the "Platinum" etc…

The big advantages is this structure is that it allows all people in your target market to access your information at their convenience and financial ability, and you can deliver multiple offerings with very little new content development. Remember you can't get paid if you're not offering information.

I have a number of discount plans I offer my corporate, agency, and individual clients. For consulting I offer discounted added services for work over my base contract; for in-house workshops I offer a flat fee for a minimal group of attendees, and an additional low fee for each added attendee. registrations.

 If there is not a minimal amount of attendees the agency receives credit to any of my public workshops for an indefinite period of time for those seats. For my public workshops I offer pre-payment with a built in discount; for individual registrations I allow all to attend any scheduled program as opposed to locking them into one date.

Bundling

Along with repurposing your expertise into many different formats you can also bundle the formats into dozens of options for the buyer. You can customize or provide set "bundles."

Be creative. It always amazed me that on the same shelf in the appliance store you could buy a crock pot that would cook your food in twelve hours or right next to it a microwave oven that can cook the same food in five minutes.

Netflix has stayed up with the fast paced technology by offering DVD's to be mailed to your door, or watch the same movie or show online on their web site. You can now watch a Netflix video on your Wii. They also aggressively figured out an effective and efficient strategy to not only compete with the corner movie store but run them out of business. Walmart is now selling pharmaceuticals and having them delivered to your door through a partnership with FedEx.

Additional Profit Centers

There are as many other sources of income for your intellectual properties as your creativity can design. Consider:

Who else has the same mission and message as you?

- Affiliations
- Partnerships
- Sub-contracting arrangements
- Sponsorships
- Distributorships
- Licensing agreements
- Certification program with an educational institutions

Whether it is a tele-conference, or live speech, the audience should always perceive that they are benefiting from the opportunity of purchasing CD's, books, and other informational products plus a free added value related gift.

Chapter Six

Consult as You Speak

Why Consult?

You have used your unique professional expertise to solve thousands of issues and problems in your past jobs. You have applied Effective approaches in helping your colleagues, patients and clients toward solving problems and issues. You have been a consultant all along.

Consulting is just another fancy name for what you have been doing all these years in your organization. When your boss asked you for your opinion, you were an internal consultant, when other departments asked you for your expertise, you were an inter-departmental consultant.

Great consultants are always problem solving three steps ahead of the discussion. Some of best politicians and leaders are renowned for this skill.

As we mentioned earlier, consultants are experts who get paid for asking the right questions, and provide the correct solution based on the client's answers. Consultants can be involved with an organization for one day or up to many years. They could be providing feasibility studies, strategic planning, project implementation, training, quality assurance oversight, evaluation pieces, or all the above.

A great consultant is skilled to anticipate the problems and provide the solutions before situations happen with the client's systems.

The Big Benefits of Consulting

As with speaking there are many benefits as a healthcare consultant. They include:

- Controlling your own schedule

- Setting your own fees

- Determining what tasks you do and don't want to spend time performing

- What environments you do and don't want to work with

- Controlling your travel schedule

- Decreasing stress of a traditional workplace

Where Can You Consult

Don't leave money on the table as a speaker or trainer. You are functioning as a consultant before and after your presentations. Get paid for all you do. Don't just stop there. Ask the client what else you can do for them to "heal their pain, or solve their problem." besides a presentation? Any additional paid activities other than your presentation are considered *consulting work*. There are several activities and skills you can offer to clients with problems.

Five specific types of clients you can approach:

1) Individuals needing information relating to their health or the healthcare industry

2) Individual healthcare practices or organizations that need professional advice on profitability or productivity

3) Healthcare agencies or networks that need professional service or advice

4) Healthcare associations requiring your presentations, workshops, licensed materials or advice

5) Non-healthcare organizations and associations wanting your advice, information and informational products and services

The services and informational products that particularly can be offered to the above five are:

- Analyzing and correctly identifying their problem
- Writing proposals
- Researching solutions
- Designing and implementing solutions
- Evaluating successful solutions
- Writing grants (and including yourself in the implementation of the work)
- Writing "Request For Proposals" (RFP's – especially private and government funding sources)
- Formulating and writing policy
- Designing and performing audits
- Managing credentials preparation
- Writing operational manuals
- Providing public relations and promotional campaigns
- Designing and delivering training programs
- Providing professional services (financial, legal, etc.)

The Secret Skills and Techniques of Successful Consulting

The key competency of a consultant is asking the right questions. The second most important is effective listening (not just hearing). A good consultant anticipates problems, develops preventive plans and solutions and recommends corrective preparation and activities.

Find out what your client is doing wrong. How can you help? What is their problem? What do you need to know about their problem? Make a site visit, interview personnel, perform a time and work study, deliver recommendations, implement the work. Ask your clients, "What would you like to see happen (outcome)?"

Listening and information gathering are key to effective consulting. If a client complains – don't disregard as them being unreasonable – listen – be open and flexible to evaluating and changing or customizing your process.

The science based techniques and principles you should consider besides speaking and providing leveraged informational products are:

- Survey techniques
- Questioning techniques (Socratic)
- Interviewing
- Assessing problems
- Negotiating
- Selling
- Combinations of the above

Keys to Profitable Proposals

Proposals are generally in written form and are generated because of a request from an individual or organization. In the healthcare industry these can be from individual private foundations, government agencies, professional associations, or universities and medical centers. They are called grants, request for proposals (RFP), or agreements.

The traditional sections of the proposal you will submit are:

1) Title page – RFP/Grant/Project name and identification markings, date, your contact information

2) Background – addressing the problem

3) Your goals, objectives

    a. Deliverables – action and descriptive verbs. Deliverables can include specific time quality and quantity measurements of designed materials, licensed intellectual properties, implementation steps, customization, training, promotion (of finished work), and support.

4) Methodology, outcome measurement processes, timeline, personnel, budget, and resources, standards of practice.

5) References, biographical sketch, past work

6) Costs, budgets, payment arrangements

7) Appendices

A key factor to keep in mind as you respond to the proposal is that the funder is looking for very specific and concrete deliverables. Don't try to wow the funder with extraneous information and deliverables or try to change the rationale and purpose of the proposal. Stay on message, be focused, be concise and you will increase your chance of being considered by the funder. As I mentioned earlier it is not illegal or unethical to call the funder and meet with them in order to clarify the intent of the proposal. Consider this interview an opportunity. Many times the funder will sponsor a bidder's conference that you can attend.

One of the biggest tips I can give you is to answer the questions in the proposal directly. If the question is, "Do you have an office?" answer, "Yes I have an office." You don't need to tell them the color of your walls, size of your desk or number of gigs in your computer. If they want to know they will ask. They will probably have a team of reviews using a "key point's guide." The reviewers will first look for key points that should have been directly answered. Secondly they look for creative, state of the art and complete plans you are submitting to solve their problem.

I always put myself in their shoes as I write my responses. I suggest you do the same. Imagine, for example, if you won the lottery and wrote a proposal to pay someone to decrease diabetes in a specific neighborhood of five thousand persons. What and how would you like the returned proposal to read? You would probably like to know the respondents:

- Background, qualifications, past work

- The methods and approaches they will use to implement the project

- Their ability to deliver your expected outcomes

- Agreeing to the conditions of the project

Basics of Writing Agreements and Contracts

Agreements and contracts are an acknowledgement of an outcome between the client and yourself and/or your agents. Both parties must sign the document after all final negotiations. They generally are legal documents with good and bad consequences. We always want to avoid the bad consequences. They usually fall into four categories – loss of money, unpaid spent time, incorrect standards of practice and educational or physical liability. If you can develop a template set of agreements then do so. Have an attorney review the final version. Although we always want to be client oriented, never let the agreement or contract that you have written penalize you for any negative issues.

Consider the same consequences for an agreement or contract generated from the client. You are in business. You want to maximize any and all benefits for the client. For example your speaking fee is not the only benefit you can gain from a gig.

When negotiating terms

- Go in with a win-win.
- Although the core response to any new situation is emotional, remember the first one to react emotionally loses. l
- Identify your lowest acceptance terms; do not settle for less

Other benefits include:

1) Being able to sell your books, CDs and materials to the group

2) Obtaining an email list for further contact and promotion to the group

3) Obtaining booth space at their conference(s)

4) Linking your web site to their web site

5) Obtaining a free print ad in their newsletter or magazine

6) Receiving testimonials that may be used in all your promotional efforts

If the client has negative consequences (which they will) in their written agreements, then you probably will have to agree to them. Just as your agreements or contracts are not etched in stone, neither is theirs. Their computer keys work magic just like yours. If you don't agree with their terms then you have three options. The three options are to not take the gig, take the gig and agree with their terms, or negotiate. Always go with negotiating. If the terms (before or after negotiation) are within reason you should take the gig. If the terms are undesirable, especially after negotiation, then do not take the gig! In my experience the relationship and situation will probably only get worse. So run – run fast!

The general components of your agreement or contracts should include:

- Scope of work (each specific action)

- Conditions (environment, travel, impacts on your work, cancellation, etc...

- Standards (the quantity, quality, and comparison entities the work will meet)

- Time allotments (per whole project and each action or task)

- Payment, fees, (taxes, etc..) amounts and schedule

- Use and limitations of your intellectual properties

- Client support and contribution(s)

- Additional benefits (as mentioned above)

How to Set Fees

The determinants for your fee should never include an hourly rate. Your (unique) value, client need, and market competition should drive the established fee. What can you live with? I learned a long time ago that if I don't get the fee I want and rave reviews from the audience, I get very sad. I don't like to get sad. I make sure I get the fee I want and prepare well to get those rave reviews. I could not have lasted in this business for over twenty years if I consistently hadn't received both rewards nearly 100per cent of the time.

Time is a friend and an enemy. It is both an asset and liability. The amount of time you should spend on a client depends on

- Amount of money you will earn from the client after expenses
- Your past and future relationship with the client
- Amount of "aggravation, energy or interruption in your work flow.

Many experienced speakers and consultants will tell you that they can sense that 'red flag' go up very early in the process of working with a client. Tip offs will alert them off that things are not going to go well.

Chapter Seven

Manage Your Business

Maximize Your Profitability and Productivity

Build and Plan with Your Best Practices

You are now ready to combine all your great experience, market research, and expert content along with business goals and measurements.

To maximize your success you will need to develop a process that will result in a profitable and productive result. By committing all your knowledge and skills, science based technology, and state of art business practices you will insure success.

This process is called developing "Best Practices."

The advantages of managing a best practice process are:

- Allows you to document results
- Incorporate the documented results in your future works
- Promote your business with measured and documented results
- Sell, license or consult your proven processes to your niche market
- Collect effective feedback
- Immediate ability to change strategies
- Increases profit
- Decreases loss of productivity
- Better time management
- Allows you to focus on growth

Some activities to consider in applying a best practice are:

- Financial goals
- Meeting your personal lifestyle goals
- Your professional growth to your skill base
- Niche market response
- Presentation acceptance
- Format salability
- Success of systems
- Promotional campaigns

Some key questions to answer in your best practice process are:

- What results will be measured?
- How will you measure results?
- How often will you assess your activities?
- Who will collect, manage, and analyze your results?
- How will you implement change?

How to Pick a Business Model

There are as many options available to you. The good news and the bad news is that it is your decision and choice; but oh so many choices:

1. Which legal structure?
   a. Sole proprietor
   b. Partnership (my advice – don't or at least ask yourself why?)
   c. Corporation
   d. Sub-contractor

        e. Affiliate
2. What scope (what market or audience do you serve)?
        a. Full time
        b. Part time
        c. Seasonal
3. Which niche?
        a. One niche – one topic,
        b. One niche – many topics,
        c. Many niches – one topic,
        d. Many niches – many topics
4. What types of services?
        a. Speaking
            i. Keynotes
           ii. Breakouts
          iii. Workshops
          iv. Web based conferences
            v. Public vs. corporate venues
          vi. Publications
        b. Consulting
            i. Short term
           ii. Long term

          iii. Coaching
5. What venue?
        a. Audience type
        b. Meeting space or site
6. What will be the extent of travel?
        a. No trips, a few trips, many trips?
7. How will you determine price?
        a. High price, low volume
        b. High price high volume
        c. Low price low volume
        d. Low price low volume

Given the above criteria, use the matrix below, to focus more towards your ideal practice model.

Design Your Ideal Model

Component	Your Choice and Description
Legal structure	
Scope	
Niche	
Speaking Services(s)	
Consulting Scope	
Venues – choices and limitations	
Travel choices and limitations	
Pricing	

Now in prose weave the above eight components into a descriptive statement of your idea practice and model.

How Little or Big Will Your Business Become?

Remember those words in the Rolling Stone's song. *"You can't always get what you want, but if you try sometimes, you just might get what you need."*

Imagine you were Donald Trump, and had all the resources you needed – what kind of practice would you want? What practice do you need? Prepare for change in scope, especially fast and substantial growth. How will you manage success, growth and change?

 Decide the size and scope you will design for your practice. There are many business models you will be able to choose from. Review the opinions below to guide you towards toward your idea business model.

Although you have an infinite number of models for your business, you really have to make a decision and choose one. Consider the time and energy that you want to commit. You can deliver one presentation a year or over two hundred as I do. You can deliver these from your own home (over the phone and/or internet), in your own town or city, nationally or globally. You can be a one person show with a home office or employ many people and own or rent your own office.

The scope of your practice also can take on any number of characteristics. The options are:

1. The specific opportunities that you want available for you
2. The number of speeches and presentations you want to present
3. The specific venue and location of speeches and presentations
4. Office scope
   a. home
   b. shared space
   c. rented - sole
5. staffing
   a. employees
      i. full time
      ii. part-time
      iii. per diem
6. The amount of time traveling
7. The size of audiences
8. The background and level of audiences
9. The types of speakers environments

10. The types of presentations
    a. Educating and training
    b. Entertaining and enjoyment
    c. Persuading or motivating
    d. Combination of above three

11. Purpose of presentations and benefits delivered could address
    a. Clinical
    b. Educational
    c. Community Health
    d. Management and Administrative
        i. Interpersonal
        ii. Leadership
        iii. Group dynamics
    e. Financial Combinations of contents

Planning Steps for Your Business

1) What new service or product should I be developing and to whom?

2) Who will pay my fee?

3) To whom and how should I promote myself?

For you, in your business, asking and answering these three questions, will minimize stress and anxiety and guarantee to grow your business.

Strategies for Planning Your Business

Four questions that should be but rarely are included in a business plan are:

1) How do you stay in business?

2) Can the targeted market pay?

3) How do you deal with change?

4) How will you plan to sell your business?

A business plan does not have to be a lofty or lengthy document. It should not be a tortuous task for you. You should look forward to developing clarity towards the direction you want to travel. When you plan a vacation you don't map out every meal, gas stop, or souvenir shop for the trip. You decide and confirm the most important factors of the trip, whether its airplane, auto, train or other travel plans, lodging, car rental, special shows or events needing advance reservations. You also consider a second tier of credentials such as; identification, clothing, money, medication, cell phones and contact phone numbers. You then casually consider a third tier of music CD's, books, games beach gear, etc.

Write a business plan for your enjoyment and personalized purposes. Develop a vision statement based on your dreams and values. Devise a mission statement how you will operate your business. Given your research develop your Business Plan.

In most board games like backgammon, checkers, etc.., there are three goals 1) to protect your playing pieces, 2) to move your pieces forward, and 3) to knock the opponents' pieces out of the game.

Running your business follow the same principles.

First, plan for the worst case scenario concerning legal, financial, standards of practice, client support issues, and unexpected growth.

Second, with passion, gusto, and enthusiasm develop exciting, and unique informational creations, and aggressive marketing and promotion strategies.

Third, compete within the market place by growing professionally, spiritually and socially.

As your business grows you will be able to distinguish trends in sales and income, purchasing equipment and supplies, paying employees or contractors, and sponsoring promotional campaigns.

In all the roles of our lives we can (or do) function at either: survival, maintenance, or growth level. Where and how do you want to be functioning in your practice?

The most important impact on your business is to manage and review your systems daily. This is the key to always being organized and ahead of the game.

The fastest way to take the fun and profit out of your speaking business is to feel overwhelmed and out of control. Stress, anxiety, deadlines, and inaccurate recordkeeping can take a toll on your psyche and bank account.

By implementing a number of simple systems you can not only avoid failure but guarantee success.

Start Your Business Plan

Decide on the path or approach to building your speaking practice. This is called "planning" Try not to be grandiose or long range. Write a plan that is appropriate and fits your practice scope and model.

There are a number of models and components for developing a business plan. The perfect plan is the one that works for you. Develop your own document as you build your practice.

We will write aspects of your business plan as we move through the chapters. The plan should be reviewed and evaluated every day and week and you should be open and flexible to change. It is good to have an advisory group (see "master mind" in last chapter). Be careful not to foresee tasks as strategic outcomes. Putting "purchase office supplies" in your plan is not a strategic outcome; completing "the" book is a strategic outcome. Booking "X" number of speaking engagements with certain financial gains is an outcome.

I am going to use a number of terms relative to goals, and objectives, and outcomes. I conceptualize objectives as being steps to accomplish goals. I view process steps as the activities needed to accomplish an objective or goal. Tactical activities are the "tactics" to accomplish a goal. Strategic goals are achieved through a series of tactics. These are the way I organize my thoughts and plans in running my business. Don't get hung up on my terminology. Call yours "steps, "outcomes", things…anything that works for you. Attainable short term goals build confidence as they are met.

"The most important goal for your practice is the focus and to finish the one you have scheduled in the few minutes."

Don't look beyond the horizon. Do baby steps.

I have adapted the classic business plan to fit your speaking and consulting practice:

1. Executive Summary
   a. Identified Passion
   b. Core Expertise
   c. Confirmed Niche
   d. Description of Brand
   e. Ideal Market

2. Your identified outcomes.
    a. Scope of Practice
    b. Practice description
    c. Financial plan
    d. Image and Brand

3. Mission Statement
4. Vision Statement
5. Personal Biography
6. Services Descriptions
7. Informational products Descriptions
8. Market Analysis Conclusions
    a. Niche
    b. Prime target market
    c. Sub-markets
    d. Prime target wants and needs
    e. Competition strengths and weaknesses
    f. Your Unique Value Proposition (s)

9. Promotion Strategies

10. Financial Plan
    a) Projected income
    b) Breakeven analysis
    c) Cash flow
    d) Profit and Loss
    e) Where are you
    f) Where and when do you want to be

Build and Manage Your Systems

"Systems, Systems, it's all about Systems!"

The definition of "effective" is producing a decided, decisive, or desired effect.

The definition of "efficient" is acting or producing effectively with a minimum of waste, expense, or unnecessary effort.

Eighty per cent of problems are system problems not people problems. Those people even include you. If you are experiencing problems or not finishing your goals it might not be you, but a lack of setting up a system.

One definition of "organized" is "forming into a structure, system, or coherent whole. "Systematic" is defined as ordered and planned. Both entities infer efficient and effective.

You must be effective and efficient in delivering your services and informational products as well as developing and promoting new content. Any other function or task is interfering with your success.

Information is power, but first you must find it. It is critical that you organize your paper and electronic resources so that that can be instantly recovered.

The techniques for controlling and separating your personal tasks and business tasks need to follow some sort of system.

Systems are only as good as the people that design them. Bring others into the process of developing your systems.

Systems help you to be more effective and efficient. Six systems to consider designing and managing are:

A. Office
B. Staffing
C. Legal
D. Finance
E. Audit
F. Data

A. Office Systems

For over twenty years I have had a home office. I calculate I have saved over $200,000.00 by not paying rent to a landlord and gaining a home office tax deduction. I was able to use that money towards the mortgage for my home.   I have also had the freedom and accessibility of using my home office whenever I needed to. There are options however for private or shared rented office space - single or multiple rooms.

1. Space - Whether you work in a rented, shared or a home office, the key features that support an effective and efficient environment are:
   - effective and esthetic lighting
   - controlled temperature
   - Spatially-arranged and free of clutter - clutter is anything that is not presently useful or aesthetically appealing.
   - dedicated space
   - correct equipment and supplies

2. Furniture – style, comfort, practicality
   - Desk
   - Chair
   - Credenza (extra counter/desk space)
   - Files
   - Equipment – ease of use, cost, flexibility (computer, printer, phone, media copying devices)

The following items are other options for your speaking practice

   - Land line phone
   - Smart phone
   - Four-in-one printer (Fax, phone, printer, scanner)
   - Phone head set
   - Blue tooth for cell phone
   - Microphone for recording to your computer
   - Digital voice recorder (DVC) and lavaliere microphone (recording your presentations)
   - Voice recognition typing system
   - Pad and pen (everywhere) or DVC
   - Flip video (recording interviews and testimonials
   - Docking stations
   - Router
   - LCD projector
   - Speakers (for laptop/power point presentations)
   - VCR/DVD player/recorder/copiers
   - Television monitor
   - CD/DVD player/burner
   - Digital still/ movie camera

3. Security concerns
   - Computer – use passwords; employ firewalls with your Internet services provider
   - user names and passwords – employ with bank accounts, internet and web services (change frequently)
   - Router – configure to be password protected

- Office – surveillance cameras (today's technology allows digital recording storage and/or live remote viewing)
- Online backup – continuous or timed online backup of all files for single or network computer

- Hard drive back up – server or portable units that can serve as manual backup
- Flash drive back up – more portable backup and transfer of any specific set of files

4. Files
- Electronic newsletters and resources - do not print them out. Setup a document with the category of the newsletter or resource and cut and paste it to the designated document. This will be a good central document for that topic.
- Templates – compose as many template and form letters as possible and custom them to each respondent. This is especially helpful for email

- Responses when the response is always the same but may be lengthy. This little "system' saves me a lot of time each day.
- Backup all electronic files. You can do that yourself with external hard drives, networked computers or with online backup services.
- Keep only one "idea" document – divide it into as many categories as you wish but only maintain one document. Enter those scraps of paper or dictated nuggets of wisdom at the end of every day. It will only take minutes. If you wait too long the pile will become overwhelming and they will now be a turnoff. You need to feel positive about those future ideas – they are called dreams – a must for any creativity and successful, business. Be realistic – keep them very

small – you will never get to eighty per cent of these ideas and by the time you do get to them they will either be out of date or someone else beat you to it.

5. Supplies

You are probably already like that deer in the head lights – overwhelmed with new computer operating systems, software updates, social media, smart phones, blue tooth this and blue tooth that.

Take it on faith – you will survive. Don't run away, don't lose sleep over changes, just jump in, hang in there, you will be in control and familiar with the new challenge quickly. With repetition comes success. Changes are constant and there will always be a learning curve to climb. Rely on colleagues, and experts as resources.

Part of an efficient business and office is being prepared and anticipating future needs.

Certainly equipment and supplies fall under this area. Work from a checklist that includes order points and minimizes inventory. Know your order points. Look for discounts, bulk buying, and other cost saving measures.

A major advantage nowadays are the "print and copy on demand" informational services available to us as speakers. We do not have to order hundreds of copies of our books or manuals or other productions so we have to look at them every day as they sit unsold in our garage. Online office supplies and wholesale outlets now make available economic office supplies and equipment. We can now buy a fully loaded laptop for what we used to pay for a PC monitor alone.

Consider doing all your business with one vendor. You can even join their rewards program and receive actual cash back

B. Staffing System

According to Alexander Mckenzie, an organizational development expert, the key functions of managing personnel are:

- Select
    - o Recruit qualified people
- Orient
    - o Familiarize new people with the situation (empower towards organizational buy-in)
- Train
    - o Make proficient by instruction and practice

- Develop
    - o Help improve knowledge, attitudes, and skills; (provide feedback loop communications, recognition)

For every task that enters your mind or comes across your desk, ask the question, "Who can do this for me?" Trust all to do their job. Doesn't micro-manage, but do evaluate frequently. Delegate responsibility not authority.

Don't be afraid of giving up control or delegating functions to others. Be a good manager. Especially farm out the tedious tasks and you do the ones you enjoy and have fun with. If there are still any tedious tasks you still have to do, complete them first thing during your workday.

One of the biggest inclinations and mistakes we all make is to do it ourselves. As with all living creatures, from the little amoeba to human beings, we are inclined to take the path of least resistance. That path of least resistance could be – "I can do it faster than someone else." or "I can do it better." or "It will take too long to find someone to do it."

We also might like to do the tasks ourselves so it is a safe place to be, as opposed to learning a new skill or dealing with a problem facing us that day. I sometimes will have 100-200 participants and clients per week. If left up to me, I would love to enter names and personal data in a data base and analyze that data. I find that fun. To enter 100 participants with names, addresses, email addresses, telephone numbers, name of workplaces, date of attendance, fees paid, etc. takes 1-1/2 hours. That's 3-4 hours a week I could be using to develop more speeches, written or audio/video materials or marketing my services. I have given that task up to a virtual assistant.

Shop around for your own virtual assistant. Consider E-lance.com, Craig's list or other clearing houses, professional associations, etc.

Potential Staffing Considerations

1. Financial
   a. Bookkeeper
   b. Certified Public Accountant (CPA)
2. Office
   a. Phone answering
   b. Correspondence
   c. Data entry and management
   d. Scheduler
   e. Travel arrangements
   f. Mail processing
3. Legal
   a. Lawyer
      • Business structure

- Copyright, patent, trademark
- Intellectual properties
- Negotiating fees
- Writing contracts

4. Printing and Publishing
    a. Graphic artist
    b. Printer
    c. Editor
    d. Publisher
5. Promotion
    a. Public Relations
    b. Marketing
    c. Advertising
    d. Sales representative
    e. Web host
    f. Web designer
    g. Web master
        ii.

6 Professionals Development
    a. Skills coach
7. General Vendors and Suppliers

I could write a whole book on managing your staff and vendors. The contents would conclude that you become effective:

- Recognizing and complimenting their work and accomplishments,
- Reward them additionally for their exceptional work,
- Reprimand them professionally, remembering 80% of problems are either systems or communications issues, and
- Remember, delegate responsibility not authority.

C. Legal Systems

These functions should not be performed by you. It is absolutely wise to find and hire the best advice and services you can afford.

Hire a lawyer to setup your practice structure. The options are:
- Sole proprietor -
- Partnership
- Corporation
- LLC
- Sub-contractor
- Affiliate

Other legal services to consider:

- Contracts
- Patents
- Copyrights
- Trademarks
- Non-compete
- Intellectual protection

- Regulations
- Laws

One of the best kept secrets of designing a contract is to ask the client what they want in it and what their expectations are, standards, and outcomes. Whether it is government, non-profit, or a major corporation, too many times healthcare professionals believe they should not or are not allowed to speak to the person making the decision. Quite the opposite is true.

The insurances you should consider are:

- Malpractice
- Liability
- Fire and theft
- Disability
- Educational
- Accident

D. Financial Systems

Keeping your practice from failing means you are gaining more income than you are incurring expenses. The margin of profit usually depends on the volume of services and informational products delivered. A number of clients I coach have cash flow problems because they are not covering their expenses. Usually it is because they are not providing enough services or informational products often enough. Not to simplify financial management but it's usually about the income; not having enough of it. **The worst risk to your business in not having any.**

No matter what system or model you choose to keep financial records, Set up a system from day one. It is much easier to enter a few transactions a week, instead of an over whelming amount at the end of the year. The keys to good accounting are to enter all financial transactions frequently, and analyze the data on a frequent basis.

The first principle of finance is to have something (asset) to manage. It is important how much you earn, but it is even more important how much you keep. A definition of "managing" is *controlling*. You must control the income (money coming in) and expenses (money going out).

The two big factors that optimize your financial success and control are: 1) planning ahead with realistic projections of income and strategic control of planning ahead on what and how much you will spend on overhead, and 2) frequently reviewing and the impacts on cash flow.

Base your pro forma budget on past income, your current market analysis and exact expense quotes from your vendors. Budget for only ¾ of your expected income and 1 ½ of the expected expenses. You will always end up right on budget.

Your financial system(s) should include:

- Pre-plan (pro forma of cash flow)
- Sell your services and informational products (profit centers) and pay your expenses
- Review all profit centers (speeches, products, consulting, contracts) and the impacts of the marketplace on the success or failure
- Assess weekly: respond to problems quickly and efficiently; do not be afraid or ignore the need for change. Change is part of growth and should be embraced.

Years ago we sponsored eight seminars a month in four different cities each and every month. Our average attendance at each program was 75 participants. We employed five speakers for each day. Can you imagine the planning and analysis that was needed to stay in business? Data and activities were entered, assessed and processed every week.

E. Banking Services

Eventually you will want to setup a separate checking account, merchants account (for internet sales), and savings account (SEP - Simplified Employee Pension, IRA, etc...), and lines of credit. Consider not only performing as many transactions online with one provider but also making sure the transaction can be transferred very easily into QuickBooks, or similar type software. Your accountant is the expert who can arrange an efficient system for you.

F. Taxes

What is the most important thing you need to know about taxes? As a lawyer once advised me, "Pay them."

As a rule of thumb for every dollar you earn, you should put twenty to thirty per cent of that in an account as an IRS quarterly estimated tax account.

There are a number of inexpensive software packages out there that allow you or your bookkeeper to enter all your income and expenses and tag them as taxable or not. If you do this every week or month, at the end of the year just a couple of quick steps will allow you to complete your tax forms within minutes. Hire an accountant to minimize your tax commitments and maximize your savings/investments.

G. Audit Systems

It is also critical that you set up any number of quality assurance (QA) programs. How will you know the standards you originally incorporated are still being upheld? Is your message still scientifically correct? Are your delivery systems still technically up to date? Are your presentation materials, promotional pieces and audio-visuals holding up? Are your sub-contractors, vendors and affiliates' services still meeting your standards?

H. Data Systems
"The major problem with a data management system is entering the data"

One of the most important and critical functions you will do (if not the most important) in managing your business, will be to capture and analyze information or data. Key data sources will be every single audience member, client, colleague, competitor, service provided, product sold, financial transaction and sales and promotional outcome.

Storing the Data

All information and pieces of data need to be collected and stored. You will be analyzing sales trends, cash flow and budget changes on a weekly, if not daily basis. You will need to access sales leads, clients, participants in your programs, staff and vendors, not only for trend analysis but personal information.

Your data storage systems should be setup so a stranger could come in, find and understand your business in a short time (they call this an audit.) Electronic software abounds. A database and spreadsheet will meet all your needs. Don't be afraid of this type of software. Although there is a learning curve, continuous use will turn you into a real propeller head. You know the old saying in healthcare, "If it's not documented, it didn't happen." So capture the data, store it, and setup frequent queries to analyze your trends. Try to document all activities in as many ways as possible. Do not miss an opportunity to obtain email addresses, survey questions or referrals from every one you meet. Enter the data into the most separate pieces possible. It will be much easier and more versatile to sort and analyze this way.

Have the data entered as soon as possible. Follow up on all data sources immediately

Analyzing Data

Setup a method to analyze your "Metrics." Metrics refers to identifying quantifiable data and analyzing that data to assess performance. The performance could be financial, attendance, market response, or sales. Recruit objective and experienced personnel to assist you in the analysis of the data. Use the results of your analysis to find problems in your planning, react to the market, and develop new services and products.

It is called "data management" not "data fear." Don't be afraid of the technique or work involved in entering and analyzing your life's works. The payoff is immense!

Supporting Your Systems with Effective Problem Solving

Once you have your systems in place and monitor them, you will want to react to change by implementing sound problem solving techniques:

The Problem Solving Model

- Define problem
- Set number one priority
- Express measurable behaviors and set time lines
- Define goal that can be controlled
- Action plan – small steps
  - Create accountability
  - Defined time for measurable concrete output
  - Implement
  - Reassess, choose second choice, repeat the process

Chapter Eight

Managing Yourself

Personal and Professional Organizational Skills

Managing a successful healthcare speaking practice is all about taking care of details to accomplish the big outcomes. Usually it's the little things that change our life. *"If you count your pennies the dollars will take care of themselves"*

Our life path is paved with the choices we make. Success or failure just doesn't happen one day. Each follows a process. Which process will you setup for yourself?

Being prepared and organized in your professional and personal activities minimizes mistakes and expenses. Being organized saves you time and money. Successful speakers work smart, not hard.

Professionally we need to be efficient and effective to maximize success. Organization is all about anticipation. Anticipate opportunities or problems in your practice and plan to capitalize the result in a positive outcome. You may choose to "organize" yourself by any number of the below activities, functions, or components:

Choice	Your Check List
Administration/Finance	
Research	
Development	
Promotion	
-or-	
Spatial considerations	
Informational systems	
-or-	
Services	
Presentations	
Informational products	
-or-	
Personal Life	

Practice Owner	
Professional Life	
Recreational Life	
Spiritual Life	
-or-	
Any other activity, function or role	

Make whichever matrix you design for yourself able to identify the successful behaviors, habits, routines, negative barriers and distractions that need to be dealt with to insure reducing stress, frustrations, and disorganization.

Some of the top reasons speakers and consultants experience barriers to success are:

- Not focusing and completing a task or project
- Not prioritizing or sticking with prioritized outcomes
- Over/under judging either time or work quantity
- Poor time management and procrastination

I am the king of organization. Here are some successful interventions for the following factors that disrupt being organized. Eliminate or minimize these barriers with the listed tips and suggestions to stay ahead of your competitors.

Spending just ten minutes at the end of each day implementing a "preventive maintenance plan" for your business by planning out the priorities for the next day will guarantee a flow of success. What doesn't get planned today will not be accomplished tomorrow.

Crucial Office Routines

The U.S. Census Bureau recently reported that one half of over twenty three million businesses are operating out of the home.

a. Twenty years ago when I first setup my home office a friend of mine gave me two pieces of advice. One was to get dressed in the morning as if you were going to work, and the second one was to not turn on the television. Don't turn it on except to view work media.

b. Mail- handle once: pitch, respond or pass on. Don't pile or file if you can help it. You will never again see 80per cent of items you file.

c. Phone calls –call first thing in the morning. I have three business lines plus email to review.

d. Perform the nastiest tasks and projects first; do the fun projects last

e. I will return all calls the same day including calls on my caller id from those who did not even leave a message.

f. Email – answer all clients and customers by phone as opposed to a return email. It is an opportunity for relationship building and to assess their needs.

g. Do not print out any emails. Instead copy, date and paste the email to a designated electronic document in a specific folder.

h. Be neat. My little quirks are having nothing on the floor and separate piles for each topic area.

i. Keep old food out of the office (fresh snacks allowed and encouraged)

j. Combine like tasks – great time saver

k. Protect Creativity Promotion Time

Intimate Informational Management

a. Files
      1. Extra storage
      2. Date every note or reference you log.
b. Lists
c. Books
d. Magazines
e. Library
f. Hardware
g. Software
h. Data - Back up the last documents and data you have worked on – windows list these files for you on "start" menu under "recent items"

No Clutter Zone

Clutter is anything that is not presently useful, or aesthetically appealing.

Heed the formula C+D=S + BF

(Clutter plus Disorganization = Stress and Business Failures)

a. A big step towards designing a clutter-free looking work space is to keep files and piles and <u>all</u> off the floor. If nothing is on the floor than it has to go on a table or desk top. When those piles get unbearable you will act to straighten clutter.
b. Keep your piles separate and sort, file, pitch or apply daily.
c. Keep your space spotless. The neater your space is the less stress and angst you will experience, and the more creative and productive you will be. There are many scientific studies that conclude a messy space is not conducive to your success.

d. Eliminate all little unrelated tasks. Block off sacred time to write, or market. Possibly divide each day by function.

Controlling Your Attitudes and Emotions

Life really is an attitude. Keep it positive. It is an art to do so. Surround yourself with positive people, environment, books, TV programs, etc...

a. The two things all human beings are experts at are rationalization and passive avoidance. Get frequent feedback from colleagues, family, coaches, and/or counselors.
b. If the task does not get accomplished ask yourself, "Why?" Analyze what isn't working for you to get your valuable
c. outcomes accomplished. When you are successful, ask yourself what accounted for the success?
d. Work ethic – what is it and how do you develop it? Set small doable tasks that will develop into a habit. This really is the secret to establishing discipline. Repetition. Staying motivated is the treatment for fighting "laziness."
e. Be careful about saying, "I'm going to do this and I'm going to that," etc. We are all wired for procrastination. Don't just talk about it -just do it.
f. Get over your fear of success.
g. Get over total altruism. Take care of others, but take care of yourself and your business as well.

Meeting Your Personal Needs

a. Designate one day a week as a personal day. Treat yourself. Relax.
b. Enjoy some form of regular exercise. With the advent of Wii and other interactive games you can maximize your enjoyment and keep coming back for more.
c. Separate personal tasks during work hours – be very careful not to pay bills, write personal emails, sort magazines, etc. during your "office hours." This usually is a sign of passive avoidance from marketing or content development tasks.

Travel Tips

When traveling, prepare by using an items checklist. Consider scheduling most of your travel arrangements with one source. A travel agency that you have a personal relationship is best. If you are using on-line services shop around for the best deals, they change hourly.

Arrange for access to all your banking and web based codes and always obtain the home, cell and business number of your contact person, airline, hotel and fellow travelers. Don't ever check luggage containing things you can't lose.

Stress Management for the Professional Speaker

I have found that the greatest stress in managing a speaking and consulting practice is knowing that you are <u>not</u> going to address a problem or task.

Stress is defined as "our bodies" reaction to change that requires a physical, mental or emotional adjustment or response."

The "good stress" is said to be our internal "fight or flight" response. Through thousands of years of evolution we have developed this physiologic ability to instantly respond to danger, confrontation or challenge. This is said to be "good" because it is part of our internal survival system. Our bodies respond and cope appropriately to this primeval need.

If however we are confronted with long term and lower danger situations we are given the choice on how we will cope. Unfortunately we generally choose the wrong coping mechanism.

80per cent of physical illness is caused by stress or in fact the way we deal with stress. We choose to cope with cigarettes, food, alcohol, sedentary lifestyle, etc. Five of the top seven killers of adults in the United States are caused from 5 or 6 bad coping choices.

The common mental and emotional stressors that we respond to with bad coping choices are anxiety, anger, depression, loneliness, boredom, frustration, and a sense of lack of control. These emotions can be in our personal and/or professional roles.

In a recent survey, here is a list of some of the key causes of stress that have been reported to me by health industry professionals:

- Not prepared to speak (not knowing content and/or audience)
- Feeling overwhelmed
- Perception of lack of control

- Cash flow problems
- Unknown financial status
- Returned phone calls hanging over their heads
- Returned emails needed to be returned
- Too many emails in their mail account
- Data not entered into a data source
- Data and paper files piling up
- Not finding supplies, files, or equipment because they didn't put it back where they could find it the next time.
- Office clutter
- Information overload
- No daily exercise
- Erratic meals in the home (office)
- Not delegating effectively
- Not producing outcomes

A long time ago I figured out my worst job related "demon." It is feeling I have not been productive. I am haunted if a project is hanging over my head or if I think I am going to miss a deadline. Putting things off is maddening. As I was once told by an old boss, "You are going to have to do the task eventually, so why not now?" At the time I thought that was a little arrogant but I got the point.

We will be experiencing or anticipating problems our whole lives. We will never be without a potential problem on the horizon. It is called life. As human beings we are built to anticipate and remove problems. This is what makes us unique from all other creatures. Expect it, accept it, solve it, and move on.

Dealing with Speaker Stress

If any of the situations or roles in our lives are not well, we always have three options to remove the unwanted circumstances.

The first two are pretty straight forward:

1. Leave – we can leave a bad relationship, job, or environment and solve the problem.
2. Change – we can stay and either negotiate or command the change we need.

The problem however lies in the third choice:

3. Coping – if the situation dictates that we must stay and cannot change the conditions then we must "cope" somehow.

There really are only three categories of coping:

1. Healthy physical response

With regular exercise, healthy food choices, adequate sleep, yoga, isometric stretching and recreational diversion, we can generally stem back the tide of stress and unpleasantness.

2. Third party" support

We are lousy problem solvers by ourselves. We are designed to live in a society – we are social animals. We need other human contact, support, counseling, and coaching to more accurately move through the problem solving model. .

3. Mental Adjustment

It is said that we use only 10per cent of our brain and that includes the ability to control biorhythms and affect stress on our biological functions and thus physical disease. The use of guided imagery, visualization, meditation, hypnosis, and other forms of mental adjustment can go a long way in minimizing the "bad" stressors in our lives.

Additional Solutions of Dealing with Speaker Stress

Enjoy the challenging moments, especially in professional situations that you can control. Although we as humans don't like confrontation, we do like challenges. Enjoy the journey in building and promoting your healthcare speaking and consulting practice.

Stress usually is not easily identified and comes and goes.

Don't jam yourself up by scheduling too many activities in your day or week. You probably know friends or colleagues who are continuously late for every meeting or event you attend.

A way to minimize stress is to complete tasks as they occur and try not to let them build up. The task is going to have to be accomplished sometime, so why not now?

Answer all calls and deal with paperwork as soon as possible in the same hour or day.

There are innumerable factors that impact our real and perceived level of controls. Blunders and disorganizations of personnel in our client organizations can affect our efficiency. For example: your contact person might not submit your invoice in a timely manner or they may not make all the venue arrangements for your presentation. Learn to prepare for the unexpected. Murphy's Law will always rear its ugly head. See it as a challenge to have counter tactics ready to go.

Robert Ringer wrote in his original book entitled, *Winning through Intimidation,* that it is not the enemy you know, or the two-faced colleague that will take you down, but the incompetent person who will give you the most problems.

Avoid deadlines! Play a mind game and cut your deadline period in half. Shoot for the earlier time, and if you miss that you are still in good shape. Always being under the gun decreases the quality of your work and spoils and good feelings you would have had for the finished outcome. Give yourself plenty of time and enjoy!

How to Roll With Change

Change is hard, especially when it is not planned. Expect, welcome and prepare for change. If we are ready for changes that occur inside and outside our business then we will always succeed. Another phrase for the word change is called "life-happening." Life is not static. Millions of variables affect our lives every day. We all function in any of the roles in our lives at one of three levels: 1) survival, 2) maintenance, or 3) growth.

Effective Time Management

Any percent of accomplishing a task is better than 100per cent of wishes.

By definition and by common belief, time management is the process of maximizing productivity. For the most part we are motivated to be productive, and day to day or hour to hour to work fairly effective towards that end.

Most of us don't have a problem with time but rather with "focus management."

Philosophically we all have the same amount of time available to us daily, weekly, and monthly.

Hopefully we "plan the work, and work the plan" to the best of our ability. It is how we plan each sub- task with the correct amount of time needed for each small task that dictates you will complete the larger project.

The problem comes in when we can't focus and stay on schedule towards our goals.

There are three dear people in my life who I have known for over 30 years, who are always chronically late. The common factor among all three is that they schedule (or try to schedule) 1-2 extra stops throughout the day that are humanly impossible. Consequently probably most of the other stops for the day are not accomplished to the potential of each of those persons. So it's not time we need to manage. It marches on. It's the expectations, staying focused on our outcomes for the day that should be accomplished in a certain period. There are three key reasons they are always running behind 1) they have watched too many episodes of "Star Trek" and think Scotty is going to beam them up between meetings, 2) they don't account for travel time, and 3) they schedule just one or two more appointments in their schedule that makes it impossible to do justice to each.

The importance and benefits of effectively focusing is to finish projects and meet goals. These goals should be the parts of your business plan which in turn will make you more productive and profitable.

It is important to include this section because one of the biggest problems for speakers is their management of finishing projects and meeting deadlines.

In order to implement you're speaking practice business plan:

- Focus on one project at a time
- Design your goals to be:
  1. measurable
  2. achievable
  3. attainable
  4. realistic

- Each goal should have one action, specific standards and condition
- Plan and review your plans daily

Prioritize all your tasks and projects by three stages:

1. Must be accomplished now!
2. Should be accomplished soon
3. Would be nice to accomplish

Here are some suggestions for you for successfully finishing your big projects. Let's say that you have six big projects on your planning schedule. The first thing you need to do is to start with a draft of a completion date. Next, title each project and list all the sub tasks for each. Then assign an amount of time to each sub task and times that by 1 ½. Next add up all the sub times and see how much time for each project you will need. Now assign a completion date for each project based on the amount of time and the priority status of the project.

Here are the best and faster tips regarding focusing and time management. We have no options in managing time. It is what it is – 24 hours in a day. We really have a problem with "focus management." Meet your goals in a timely manner,

At one time I did have six projects I needed to finish. Each day I would look at those projects, and think, "I will finish all these this week." Maybe I would do a little of one or another, and kept hoping the magic fairies would finish the work for me. They never showed up. So finally I applied the above system, and discovered that the total for all the projects was 345 hours. At 40-60 hours a week this would take 6-10 weeks. I prioritized the projects by a realistic completion date, scheduled the sub tasks on a daily basis, combined some like tasks, delegated every little thing that could be accomplished by someone else (and probably better than me) , and stayed focused. It took me 5 weeks to finish all! I planned well and stayed disciplined and focused.

A simple example would be if you are using an LCD projector in your presentation and are finished, you would pack, taking time to assure that all cords, attachments, etc.., are packed. Another simple example is that if you are returning from an out of town presentation, you would pack your toiletries kit et al, so it is ready when you open it up on the next trip. This would be the time to replace any items that ran out. Another example would be to enter all financial and statistical data daily or weekly in the appropriate electronic or paper file. This would eliminate losing the information or scrambling at the last minute to retrieve and/or analyze the data. It comes back gain to that concept of being organized and thus effective an efficient.

You will be inclined to say to yourself, "Tomorrow I will work on one chapter of my book," or "I will setup a database for prospective clients," or "I will write up a description of my informational services for my website." More than likely that goal will not be met if you don't have a plan. The plan should consist of five steps: 1) Analyze approximately how much time (in minutes or hours) it will take, 2) Block out the time in your schedule for the day, 3) Be disciplined and do not let any distractions interfere with this time block, 4) Allow "wiggle room" in case unexpected interruptions occurs, and 5) Do the most important and dreaded tasks first.

CHAPTER NINE

It's All About The Marketing

"The answer is always no if you don't ask"

What is Promotion?

Two key tenets of marketing are: 1) you have to put your expertise into action (sell) – so promote, and 2) you must continuously measure the financial results of your promotion and marketing efforts.

Your speaking practice is nothing without audiences and clients. It is now time to advance and promote your well-oiled machine out into the marketplace. You will now unveil yourself, your presentations, speeches, products, and services to your identified markets. The main purpose will be to stay in business by realizing a net profit.

You will make money through sales. However, to reach those sales you must first perform a mix of marketing, advertising, and public relation and the sales functions. You must put these four specific domains into a "Promotional Strategic Plan."

You will have the ability to promote yourself in these domains through personal, print, electronic and web based vehicles. As you promote yourself to the clients and audiences, you will see a reoccurring theme in this section. Marketing and Promotion are all about relationship building.

Although "snail mail" has a bad reputation and the internet is on the top of the world for promotion, a combination of both is synergic – more powerful together than just one.

The hallmark and basis for all strong relationships is trust. Develop and communicate your vision so that it aligns with your client and audiences and you will be successful.

Promotion activities must be ongoing. The goal is to keep you and your speaking and consulting services and informational products constantly in the minds of your clients and audiences. The promotion campaigns need to effectively stimulate demand and sales.

You will attain the exact level of success that you set for yourself. Your professional self-image will be a fulfilling prophecy. There is no great conspiracy out there determined to make you fall short of your goals. The conspiracy is you. We have all come from an altruistic healthcare profession and industry where our internal focus is immature regarding profit, business and self-promotion. No one but yourself is going to promote you unless you are paying thousands to a public relations and advertising agency to do so.

There are clients and audiences out there who need your expertise and information just as badly as your patients, clients and agencies did.

Change that old attitude, get aggressive, be hungry and stay hungry. Plan and implement a promotion campaign that will allow you to provide these badly needed services and informational products to your market.

The easiest way to increase and maintain clients and audiences is to focus on one guiding statement through your promotional efforts.

As a partner in your clients and audience's successes, how are you going to help them to be more profitable or productive?

What is marketing?

Marketing is defined as the process or technique of promoting, selling, and distributing a product or services. The key marketing tasks you have already reviewed are: 1) research, 2) branding, 3) product development, 4) pricing and 5) designing your presentation and publication formats.

You are responsible for your businesses promotion. You are a promoter.

There are three remaining functions to discuss – Public Relations, Advertising, and Selling.

Public Relations

Public Relations is defined as the process of putting forward your speaking and consulting practice to not only your target markets but the general public as a whole. The goal of a good public relations campaign is to establish and maintain the goodwill and understanding of your brand.

There are many ways to provide public relations for your practice.

Consider using the instruments in the chart as promotional vehicles for your practice. How many more can you add to this chart?

METHOD	FEATURES	TECHNIQUE
Social Media	Fast, comprehensive Can send all at once along with your blogs	Linkedin, Twitter, Facebook
You	You are the best promotion for your practice.	Go see your clients; use the phone – avoid email; call your audiences
Word of mouth	20/50	"we tell 20 other people good things we experienced, 50 people bad things we experience (don't be the bad)
Print and Web Press Release	Submit to local, regional press	Use press release format
Public Service Announcement	Free; print or electronic	Build relationship with editors
No Fee Speakers Bureau	Third party promotion	Sign up with their agencies
Your Blogs	Write up most interesting and relevant; use as core content for your writings; signature stories	Log all daily activities (diary); salient helpful information
Other's Blogs	Boosts your web exposure	Find through Google alerts; respond to other's; embed your web

		address
Professional Association Contribution	Strong networking, relationship building and keeping current with standards	Know your time limitations, stay involved
List with helpareporter.com	Connects you with reporters	Sign up and submit your information
Testimonial written releases	Increases your validity and networking	everywhere you speak or consult; include in all your materials
Conference /convention booths	Mainlined networking and exposure	Attend, network, sponsor a booth or session
Media kit	Concise promotional tool	Print or electronic forms
Special events	Share your mission and message	Be a sponsor, exhibit, speak
Negotiated fee replacements	Keeps you in the "game"	If lower fee, negotiate for booth, mailing list, other gigs, etc…
Target market publications	Increase your exposure	Find out what they read – submit article, negotiate article with pay
TV interviews	Largest audience reach	Cable, web, network options
Talk Shows	Largest audience reach	Cable, web, network options
Celebrities	Recruit as sponsor or spokesperson	Recruit for niche nonprofit assoc. recruit next for

		your practice
Host your own radio or TV show	Web as well as cable	"Buy" the hour get sponsors
Holiday	Own your own holiday, week or month. Promote your practice with events, co-sponsorships, etc...	"Theme of the week"
Specialty items	Gives you long term visibility	Be creative and different. What can you give someone with your name on to that they will not throw away?
Chat rooms	Networking and promotion of your services and informational products	Only use valid professional sites
Online surveys, polls	Frequent use especially regarding your speech, product or service	Stay current with niche, design to discover new needs from you niche
Contests	Allows you align with almost any related entity in your niche	Provide giveaways as a fund raiser for non-profit organization in your niche or to award clients with a change to win your informational products or services
Web bookmarks	Store as a	Spend time daily

	resource or network opportunity	searching for relevant sites
Hold meetings at special venues	Increases your stature	Combine with nonprofit fundraisers, contents, awards ceremony, your workshops, etc…
Send notes out immediately after gig	Hand written, personalized	Have support staff assist
Articles and opinions to chat rooms and e-newsletters	Increases your visibility on the web	"Write early, write often"
Press Conference	Promote a unique newsworthy feature of you and your practice	Use prudently. Design a "lead up" strategy and timeline

Try this exercise

What if you were throwing a book signing party for your new book? You wanted to invite everybody you ever knew- people from high school, armed services career, college, sports teams you either played on or coached, church and community groups you were active with, extended family, friends, work colleagues, etc..

Name at least twenty methods **guaranteeing** their attendance:

METHOD	METHOD
1.	11.
2.	12.
3.	13.
4.	14.
5.	15.
6.	16.
7.	17.
8.	18.
9.	19.
10.	20.

Fifteen Future Funders

Although the public relations (PR) instrument is about an activity or service that you provide. Make the message always to and about the client. Here are some additional helpful hints to put your marketing efforts over the top.

1. Embed the benefit in all your speaking practice PR – "How will this help the client be more profitable or productive?"

2. Given your budget and time, consider delegating some or all the work to a PR consultant. It is critical that you realize public relations specialists cannot guarantee you book more gigs, or sell more products through their efforts. It is generally impossible track. You can however negotiate a fee to them based on concrete placements such as articles in magazines and professional journals, interviews on TV and radio shows, mentions in the print press, etc... You may also elect to pay them for tasks such as writing press releases, copy for advertisements, or interview preparation.

3. You will grow faster and become more accepted if you can refer to positive references from your past work.

4. Literally every time you speak, consult, or coach one or more individuals, get a testimonial. A testimonial should contain the following statements; a) thank you for your current work, b) a description on how your expertise helped the client or audience member.

5. Include your contact information on every promotional instrument, product, and service you provide.

6. Always measure the impact or outcome of your PR efforts.

7. Make sure that, besides the web, there is someone and/or something promoting you 24 hours a day, 7 days a week somewhere.

8. Be more aggressive than your competitors. That won't be hard. The good news is that if maintaining a great PR campaign was so easy everyone would be doing it. Most of your competitors are not organized or aggressive enough to manage a PR campaign. The advantage is up to you.

9. Always write about yourself in the third person.

10. Use the traditional format when writing press releases.

11. Always be visible.

12. Manage multiple exposures. Keep casting your net. This should be become habitual and painless.

13. Keep in touch with original contact person even if they delegate to their subordinate

14. Include statistics about yourself and practice in your promotion.

15. Can include a tele-conference call to a group book club or master mind group to discuss you book.

What is advertising?

Advertising is defined as the usually paid action of calling something to the attention of the speaking and consulting markets. An advertising campaign should be well thought out and very strategic. If your advertising activities are not coordinated and planned you can end up with very little sales, and lose valuable capital.

There really is only one purpose of advertising and that is to sell. There should be a predictable, measurable, and proportionate return on your cost of advertising to sales. Advertising is a very strategic process.

The steps of a good advertising campaign are:

1. Identify your precise markets.
2. Absolutely confirm to a 100per cent confidence that the service and informational products are needed by your markets.
3. Design your advertising components so they are appropriate and appealing to the market.
4. Know exactly where you draw the attention of your markets. Give them what they asked for and promote the key benefits.
5. Be timely in notifying your clients and audiences of your offerings.
6. Build in measurement and follow up in all advertising tasks.
7. Don't compare yourself to competitors who are more experienced or less experienced than you. Be careful not to blend in with the crowd. Even though you might have the same message as your competitors, your clients are going to

8. Pay you for how you deliver the message. Position yourself to be special and unique.
9. Make it totally clear of what you selling to who

There are many means and activities that can be part of a strategic advertising campaign are:

The Importance of Personal and Professional Promotion

You are in the business of selling services and informational products. They are the vehicles through which your clients will buy your information. You are the advertisement and promotional tool there to make the sale.

Call me old fashion but I think it is more effective to actually pick up the phone and talk with another human being as opposed to sending an email. While Email Service Providers (ESP) allows you to send bulk emails to all your clients, there is nothing like the personal touch of a phone call. Individual phone calls are time consuming, but if scheduled correctly you can make a few calls a day and call your entire client base over a very short period of time.

It's your attitude, personality and caring spirit that makes you successful. Be controversial and exciting.

Would you buy from you? How are your personal organizational skills, timeliness, persona and appearance? What could you do to be effective on a personal level?
.
Sponsor a speaker phone call to book clubs or master mind meetings and discuss your information with a whole group. This could be no fee or fee based.

Personal Promotion Strategies

1. **Word of mouth** – This is the best method of advertising. It has been said that if you have had a good experience you will tell 20 people, if you have had a bad experience you will tell 50 people. So not only is it important to do a good job, but it is critical to not do a bad job. It is actually better to do nothing than to do a bad job. We can't stay in business doing nothing – so the only option is to not only do a good job but provide the unique value proposition every time.

2. **Elevator speech** - This is described as a method used to describe your business in one breath. An elevator speech is a description of your niche and key topic you would give within 30 seconds on an elevator before the listener left the elevator. This speech obviously can be given anywhere to anyone inquiring about your informational services and products. The key features of an "elevator speech" are to explain what is in it for the prospective client, and your benefits and features tied to the outcome for the client. How many times have you been asked to describe your business (or will be asked) in an elevator? Not too many times. You will be asked for a description in many other venues however. You don't have much time to make that sale or get your "unique value proposition" across to the listener so make it count, be effective.

3. **Affiliates** – Affiliate marketing, generally internet based, is a system by which you and/or another business reward each other for promoting and selling you or their services and informational products. Although the business should be related to your niche, they should not be direct competitors.

4. **Partnerships** – Partnerships can be more formal and closer working relationships than affiliates. Each partner will promote the others. There can be legal agreements to equally develop, deliver and promote speaking, training and informational services. The arrangement can define completing a specific event, project or product.

5. **Testimonials** – You can be promoted by your clients either in their marketing efforts and/or yours. Although the best testimonials should come for your clients, you can also include well known colleagues in your field.

6. **Clients** –Clients are a rich source of promotion and almost always overlooked. Not only can clients hire you again, but they can refer you to other in-house departments, to their colleagues, their clients, and post information about you on all electronic and print publications. However, you must ask for these benefits. *"If you don't ask the answer is always no."*

7. **Meeting planners** – There is a whole process in obtaining work and referrals from meeting planners. Meeting planners can be the lone individual in an organization who coordinates all the conferences, trainings, workshops, and consultancies. Many meeting planners work for a separate business that specializes in placing speakers for their clients' venues. You should prepare your "meeting planner packet" and forward it to the meeting planner with a follow up phone call.

8. **Group Discussions** (live/speakerphone/web based) - Combine the sales of your books, manuals, or other print information with group discussion groups. You can sponsor a free follow up teleconference to discuss your book or the sessions could be centered on their work with your manuals. You would advertise this option as a whole page in your book as well as all the other advertising avenues

Considering Professional Materials

1. **One Sheet** - This is usually a two-sided 8 ½ x 11 sheet containing a head shot of yourself, logo, background information, services and informational products with benefits and features, testimonials and contact information. Spend a little money to develop a multicolored professional piece. This piece can be used as a PDF download on your web site as well as a print piece for your media kit, or a stand-alone handout at your presentations. You will be able to promote yourself to meeting planners, associations, healthcare organizations and agencies.

2. **Business Card** - Be creative. Years ago I saw one of the most unusual business cards. The card was a piece of 35mm film. The owner of the card was a videographer. People love quick "how to" type info. Put your top tips on the back of your card. Make them want to keep the card and remember you. Recently at a conference I attended, a professional speaker shared with the audience his version of a business card which was postcard sized. On one side was the cover of his book, and on the other side his top tips and contact information.

3. **Curriculum Vitae** (CV) - This is very similar to a resume. C-V's are common in the healthcare industry and usually include all you professional works. The literal translation of curriculum vitae is "life's works." Although this should not be put into your one sheet, bulleted key points should be included. The contents of a curriculum vitae are 1) formal education, publications, scholarly and research works, employment, awards, recognitions, and professional associations. It can also be included on your web site and/or in your media kit.

You will be tempted or inclined to include everything in the whole world that you do and have done. Narrow the content

for the 1 to 3 target markets you have identified. As you grow and develop new streams of income and profit centers, you can then develop more one-sheets.

4. **Media Kit** – A print or electronic media kit is a group of promotional pieces in either print or electronic format. It is usually distributed to meeting planners, interviewers, and speaking bureaus. The kit can contain your head shot; color and black and white, C-V or resume, bibliography of written or scholarly works, one sheet, separate description of services and informational products or healthcare specialty niche tips sheet, pricing guidelines, testimonials, and recent news articles naming you or your practice. It you are sending the kit to an interviewer it will be helpful to them for you to include a set of guiding questions regarding the topic of the interview.

5. **Specialty Items** – You probably have one of these sitting on your desk right now. These are the rubber balls, key chains, calendars, tote bags, etc… that businesses pass out to current and prospective clients. The key considerations of developing these types of promotional items are costs, development time, and how effective they support and promote your brand

6. **Brochures/Flyers** - These publications are a great way to promote short or long term, one or multiple informational products and services. People read flyers and brochures bottom right to bottom left. Wide spaces are appealing. Although some expert copyrighters advocate numerous pages of copy, less is usually more.

    -   When deciding which promotional material(s) to use, consider the following
    -   Weave the benefits throughout. Be clear and direct.

- Highlight key techniques, and successful outcomes. Every time you mention price also mention the benefits. Direct all offers to the buyer.

- Make the "call to action" prominent. Provide an order form, phone number and web address so the buyer may take action immediately.

- Make the promises in the headline. Write, write, write, something (one to two paragraphs) then publish it somewhere.

- Write sales letters, newsletters, or direct mail pieces.

Copywriting Tips

1. Always lead with benefits, then features
2. Design your benefits by the problem it solves
3. Point out how you are different from your competitors
4. Stay on message
5. Call to action – make them act toward your offer
6. Keep your copy short and clear: get to the point
7. Vary sentence structure with colorful active action verbs and adjectives
8. Recruit others to proofread your copy
9. Sales letter – write as if you were visiting a client
10. Include numbers and statistics
11. Combine your promotion with promotions of your affiliates, partners, clients, etc...
12. Consider hiring a copy writer (find one on Craig's list and other similar sites)
13. Write content in advance for archives, blogs and articles
14. Watch out not to send the same article to multiple sources
15. When referring to yourself, especially in the third person, call yourself an expert
16. Contribute articles to professional magazines and newsletters

Fantastic Electronic Promotion Tips

CD and DVDs are audio and video sources that can contain any and all of every piece of your expert knowledge. As I mentioned earlier in the book it is very quick and inexpensive to produce an audio or video product. This same medium can be used as a promotional method for your business. All files can be digitalized and stationed on your or other sponsored web sites. You can also include them in E-mail lists, Internet site links and Internet mail.

The best advertising campaign is one that is consistent and multi-faceted. Do the mix, and do it often.

Learn How to Sell

Sales is a process in which you approach potential buyers and effectively promote the benefits, features, advantages, and value of your speaking and consulting informational products and services. There is a real advantage during the selling process to establish and build even stronger relationships with your clients and audiences.

The Eight Electrifying Sales Strategies

1. **Discovering** -systematically obtain all sources that will lead you to your potential clients and audiences.
2. **Approaching** -using one or a combination of the advertising and public relations strategies, connect with the potential buyer and move through the sales process.
3. **Qualifying** -differentiate and eliminate those in your target market who, for whatever reason, are not ready to buy.
4. **IAAT** ("It's All about them") - the benefits, advantages and features.
5. **Clarifying** - clear up any barrier, misconceptions or objections the client or audience member might perceive

6. **Closing** - make it a win-win. Ask for the sale. Especially reinforce your unique selling proposition.
7. **Feedback**- document why they did (or didn't) buy. Get that testimonial. Get a referral. Systemize 2-4 follow up steps.
8. **Follow up** - stay connected through further public relations and advertising strategies.

Here are some particular sales skills, techniques, and tips relative to your speaking and consulting practice. A number of these I have learned the hard way or have developed through being innovative towards getting and keeping my clients.

The Key Sales Skills

Listening is one of the most important communication skills. If we are listening, we are learning. Learning about our client's needs and their opinions are our core work. Prepare for phone calls and meetings with clients. Do your homework – know them well.

Negotiating is the trick in negotiating is to have some solutions ready to go and use for their problems.

Motivating Clients makes your passion contagious. Your audiences and clients will be a mirror image of your confidence and enthusiasm. Ask questions and wait for a response.

Overcoming Resistance Have you ever been told "yes" to everything you ever asked for? There is an age old sales formula (author unknown) that states, "For every 10 contacts, three will respond and one will buy." So there is good news and there is bad

news. You have to approach ten prospects, but you will obtain one contract. Don't take a "no" so personal. There could be a thousand reasons the buyer says no. Many are out of your control and ninety nine times out of a one hundred they have nothing to do with you.

If you do receive a "no" ask for suggestions or for a re-submission at a later date. Obtain a referral from them to one of their colleagues, and never burn your bridge. If you remain professional you will be surprised by the number of times they call you back for another project. If you never ask, the answer is always no. It is in our nature to want to be liked and to avoid rejection. The simplest way to avoid rejection is never to ask for anything, instead stand up in front of a crowd, or approach another person at a party or meeting. Today the TV and computer solves a lot of problems for a lot of people.

Passion – nurture it, don't lose it. Constantly review and develop new survey tools. Deliver value – more than they expect Don't fear success. Although it is normal to be anxious about new challenges and speaking and consulting engagements, learn to get excited and enjoy the experience.

Ask the client what their goals and visions are and then deliver a speech, product or service to partner with them in achieving their outcome. Do you see yourself as a sales person? You must first sell yourself – believe you are the expert and deliver with passion. When do you say no to a sale? Never say no (well hardly ever). In your sales pitch focus on the what – deliver the how.

People love to talk – so let them. Write an unsolicited request for proposal (RFP) or proposal – write it in the third person, proposal format to clients you know need your exact topic or service.

What is the Purpose of Your Pitch?

- Describe your practice, the services, and informational products
- Gain competitive advantage,
- Sell
- Establish relationship

Successful Sales Techniques

Setup a "Memberships" option. Maximize cash flow is to offer an organization or client a membership package. This also lends itself to "added value" concept. The benefits are that you now are the sole provider of this specific service to a particular organization or client.

Prepare for telephone and meetings with clients- perform your homework and know them well. For leads, check your old appointment books, outlook, etc. Always find out why clients did not re-hire you for future work. How do you know if your market has changed? Keep track of trends impacting on your niche. Know your niche's demographics. In order to manage your business you must "sell" to the person who has the authority of saying "Yes" to your fee. Define clear conditions regarding compensation. Be open to additional forms of value to you other than money.

Handling Cold Calling and Resistance

Cold calling – don't do it. This infers that you haven't established a want or need from the client or targeted market. Second person refers and word of mouth will be more valuable that cold calling and will save you frustration and time.

If the answer is no - ask why, get competitors name, ask for future consideration, other work, approval to send follow up letter, and be put on the mailing list. Recruit others to help you analyze market analysis. Interact with your clients at least five times.

Don't punish client with sales restrictions - be client centered

Research and develop effective techniques for overcoming resistance. The best one I have ever heard is from Alan Weiss, a business consultant, is as a client states an objection to his proposal he comes back with, "That's why you need me."

You need to be constantly assessing market and demographics. Be creative in payment options. Monitor your markets and competitors.

- Always research client first
- Form initial possible solutions
- After interviews zero in on best to worst solutions and provide outcomes
- Provide many bundled options
- Always obtain at least one referral from current client or audience members and immediately follow up
- Make a "what kind of clients do you want to attract" list.
- Spend one to two hours daily calling old and new clients
- Include your no-fee events in to your database
- Promote future informational products and services

More Sales Tips

1) 30-50 per cent of clients and audiences will buy from you again
2) Don't think of yourself as salesperson but as a promoter of your passion and expertise. Partner with the audience or client towards enjoying accomplishing their goals.
3) There are two main reasons of failure: services/informational. products not needed and poor promotional plan
4) Respect your "sales cycle." Setup a system to analyze on a continuum.
5) Watch out for the curves. Just when not looking, the market will might change.
6) Only deal with those that can approve payment (decision maker)
7) Remember – you are in business. Being in business means ending up with more money than you spent running your business. A successful business also means you earned enough money to support yourself, meet your financial responsibilities, with something left over for savings or investment.
8) Set yourself apart from your average competitors
9) "If you don't ask the answer is always no" If the client says no – you are no worse off than before you asked.
10) Recruit affiliates.
11) Develop membership models
12) When an identified target says no, they mean, "Not now or not yet."
13) Avoid pre-contemplators; move others to sale.
14) Don't expect the big one every day.
15) Don't just wait for the big ones.
16) The more you try – the more they will buy.

Crucial Internet Based Promotions

Today there are thousands of cable and satellite TV and radio stations. This world is your oyster. Jerry Williams the recognized pioneer and king of talk radio, was once asked what business he was in. His answer was, "The advertising business." Approximately sixteen per cent of programming time is advertising. Radio and TV stations sell that air time. That is their business. Obviously they need to air the other 84 per cent of time. That is where you come in. The task at hand for you and the station is to match your expertise with the listening audience.

By contacting and sending out your media kit, contacting www.helpareporter.com, and searching the web for health related programming you will hope to find a match. The good news is health care is a hot and deep topic area. You generally will experience the interview format.

I have been quoted in print and appeared on a number of TV stations in the metropolitan area in which I live. The TV stations found me through newspaper articles and speaking gigs, and the newspapers have found me through the TV appearances. For you, synergy from the dozens of sources in this chapter is the key to success.

You can also buy your own show time, usually AM or web based radio. You can provide all the programming around your practice and niche. You will pay the station for the time and you can then find sponsors to pay you for advertising, thus reimbursing you the fee you paid the station.

Just spending one to two hours a day, five days week promoting your practice using and combining multi- sources will guarantee your continued success.

The Importance of Web Promotion

Technology is here to serve us. You will need to use it to relate your market. Besides yourself, the web is the best promotional vehicle you will have in your tool box. Think of the web site(s) as a 24 hour business card.

The Magic Your Web Site Can Perform

You will need a web site to promote a successful practice. The main purpose of your web site is to sell your services and products. In today's professional world you must sponsor at least one web site.

We are still discovering unique venues and purposes of communication on the web. Over 70 per cent of all professional communication is now performed on the internet.

Three other purposes of your web site are: 1) promote your informational products and informational services to your clients and audiences, 2) deliver your informational products and informational services to your clients and audiences, and 3) to communicate with your clients and audiences. Stay focused on these purposes. Highlight your benefits, and features. List the characteristics of each service and product.

A web site is a set of pages containing text, images, audio and/or video files. The web site, which can be one or more pages, is gathered on a site which is identified by a specific internet address (IP).the site is hosted on a server. The IP address is represented to the "web world" through your distinct domain name. Your site is accessed by a distinct address called a uniform resource locator (URL). This will show up as your homepage. All web sites are on the wide world web (www), and move through hypertext transfer protocol (http).

In preparation in developing a web site you will need the following things:

Domain Name(s) Are Where it's All at

As mentioned it is important to obtain domain name(s). The name(s) you choose, buy, and own really will be your brand or image to your market and niche. Two trains of thought on choosing a name to brand yourself is with your name or with a term or terms that will describe your healthcare practice services and products. Obviously there is a third choice of a combination of the first two. I feel that especially in healthcare your name is and should be your reputation. We in healthcare, for the most part provide science based expertise. Our opinions and knowledge can literally affect people's lives. The more professional we represent ourselves the better. If you are not using your name as your brand make sure the terms you are using are not gimmicky or unprofessional.

Choosing a Logo

A logo is defined as a recognizable graphic design element, often including a name, symbol or trademark, representing an organization or product. There are many web based graphic services or local graphic artists available to design your logo for you. I have used both and am very happy with both. The cost should be between $125.00 and $250.00. Do not pay any more! Shop around.

That Perfect Head Shot

A head shot is a picture of your head and upper body. (Like the one of myself on the back of this book). Find a photographer. You should have this done by a professional photographer skilled in head shots. It is a good idea to: 1) get color and black and white, 2) various poses and clothing changes, and 3) various backgrounds. With all your vendors, check references with colleagues, friends and even obtain references from the photographer. The cost of a one-hour session can vary but usually is between $150 and $400. Nowadays with digital photography you can usually walk out of the session with a disk of your approved photos.

Picking a Web Master (Designer)

Hire someone to design and manage your web site. One of my shortcomings is I like to understand the intricacies of how things work. I like to learn how to do things. I had to learn that my job description does not include web design. My job is speaking practice manager, content developer, and presenter. You can find a web designer through colleagues, local universities or technical schools, or on E-lance.com, Craig's list or other web help sites. The web designer/master will transfer your page content (see below) and implement all needed functions. The criteria for a finished product are the goals you have set for the purpose of your web site.

Choosing a Web Host

Your web designer might want to also host your web page. You have the option to host the designed site anywhere you want. The criteria you should use to make a decision are price, stability of the web host company, backup safety of their servers, and your access to analytics, changes and blog entries on the site.

The Basics Features for Your Web Site

Traditionally the pages and components on a web site can be:

- **Home Page** – as people type in your URL or domain name, "search engines" will direct them to your "landing page" or home page. It is critical that this page (and the whole site) be very easy to navigate. Lead the visitor to one or all three of the purposes of your web site.
  This page should contain: 1) all the key words for the search engines, 2) navigational options to quickly and easily lead them to learn more and buy your informational products and services.

- **About Us** – this is where you can be shameless and write in the third person, describing all the great characteristics and accomplishments of you and your practice.

- **Informational products and services** – list all you have to offer in the many formats you have designed. Attach an easy and efficient "shopping cart" so they may register and/or purchase all you
have to offer.

- **Shopping Cart** – page(s) dedicated to processing and chronicling the payments for the cost of your services and products. Your web master can obtain a SSL certificate, and merchant account for your shopping cart.

- **Meeting Planners** – just as you have developed a print packet for meeting planners you should have a digital package.

- **Testimonials** – you may elect to have one page dedicated to testimonials from current clients or audience members and/or you may pepper the testimonials throughout your site.

- **Contact Us** - your contact information (email address and telephone number) should be at the top and bottom of every page. You will also need a contact page with your full name, address, and a "request for more information."

- **Survey Form** –you can collect a lot of information with an online survey that will support your market survey and promotional campaigns. List one to five questions asking those specifics on what they think you should provide or ways you should change your practice. I own the domain name "askdennismahoney.com." This web page serves as a one type of survey tool for me.

- **Resource Pages** – as mentioned you include PDF files as a newsletter, media kit, or free downloads. These documents will support your public relations and marketing strategies.

- **Blog** – your blog can be your web site or a page of your web site. The big benefit of blogs is that they allow you to increase your visibility to the search engines on the wide world web. With your name, embedding on other blogs, add a guide to your web offers. One suggestion for writing your content is to design the content to eventually to be a book. Don't write as if it is a diary. Include facts, tips, and technical suggestions. Answer questions. Be bold. Find new news and content from Google alerts. Blog on a regular schedule. Link to other blogs.

- **Sponsors** – Include partners, affiliates and/or sponsors not only on your web site, but in all your promotions. They also can include you in all of their promotions. Traditionally you each document and share the sales of each other's products.

- **Videos** – include a short (one – three minute) ideas of yourself as promotional and informational messages, Short videos will also increase you presence on the internet. Short videos will allow you to promote yourself to clients and audiences. By using any digital camera, whether it is a web cam, flip video camera, digital movie camera, or even your cell phone, you can transfer that "short clip" also called a file, to your computer. The computer files can be uploaded onto your web site(s), to a prospective client, or to You -Tube and other video host sites.

Additional on every page:

- Insert a "sign up for our newsletter" form on every page . You will need participants' first and last name and email address.

- Add a "send to a friend" . An important feature piece on your web site is to make sure you add a "send to a friend" link, "if you would like me to contact you", or "if you would like a free…"

- Remember this is the web - don't forget the international markets
- Add privacy policy on all pages
- Include your contact information everywhere. Be easy to reach. Give all contact info on every page.

Group Internet Services

Email Service Provider (ESP) - these are special services that will provide you with templates, data management and mass emailing in order for you to send out a very professional looking newsletter. In general you really don't want to promote to the same client or Audience member more than once a month. An ESP makes this monthly process very easy.

Search Engine Optimization

 (SEO) - SEO is actually what it says. It is the process of maximizing your presence on the World Wide Web. There are mechanisms called search engines that will look for your accumulated mention and presence on the www. The more you are "present" the higher you are ranked and listed for the world to find you in a search. Your site,

advertising and other sites are the potential spots for you to be present. You might be mentioned in a news item, in another blog, on another site as partner or affiliate. On your site you can be ranked according to the "key search words" in your text, your URL, your site menu, or embedded words in your images, the number of times your site is visited and how your visitor's tour your site adds to your web ranking. It is very important that you educate yourself plus hire a knowledgeable web master in order to optimize your site.

About Social (Media) Networking

Social networking or media is currently most popular form of reaching your niche. These web based services allow you to design a confined "web" community sharing profiles, documents, messages and business exchanges. The most popular sites relative to your business are: Linkedin, Facebook, and Twitter and YouTube. Be very careful to stay professional and not log any photos, facts or information you would not want your clients to view. The advantage of connecting with others interested in your niche is 'networking." Networking will bring more visitors to your site that will translate into more business.

Promotion Strategic Plan

The promotional strategic plan should be written to give you structure including a time line, tasks, outcomes, and needed resources. Additional to a traditional marketing plan format also consider:

Here is an example of how you can organize your strategic marketing activities for healthcare audiences and clients.

The plan should include specific expectations of your clients and audience members. (What is the exact "call to action") and identify the target markets (how will you focus on one or more segments)

Market Segment	Print	Web	Electronic	Mailing
Hospital				
Health Networks				
Non-Profit Health Agencies				
Professional Associations				
Primary Care Site				
Specialty Practices				
Educators				
Clinicians				
Counselors				
Researchers				
Administrators				

1) Schedule daily and weekly tasks using the "methods of marketing table."
2) Develop and perfect effective planning skills.
3) Don't get stuck in the process steps. Think of what you will gain and how it makes your business better off. What is the value?
4) It is critical that you "bundle and reverse bundle" all your informational products and services. Be open to new suggestions and ideas too.
5) The best promotion is you connecting with your clients frequently and asking, "What can I do for you?"
6) Don't take competition personally, but do get even by winning. over and keeping your business and winning over theirs.
7) Promotion plan has to be systematic, continuous and aggressive.
8) Give it all away. Sell everything; all your expertise. What are you saying it for?
9) The "Yearly 17" contacts system – fill in on calendar.
10) Never promote to your clients more than once a month.
11) Have a special "recognition" on email service providers (ESP). such as Constant Contact or others for clients and associates...

12) Initiate the promotional timeline.
13) "Backgammon" – protect your business, move forward, and beat your competition.
14) Do one promotional task a day...
15) Setup a systematic daily, weekly, monthly approach.
16) Design your marketing to bring in the desired amount of income.
17) Evaluate sales data weekly.
18) Use sales analysis weekly.
19) Do not lose contact with your clients for more than two months

Promotional Takeaway Points

If you:

- are passionate about your expertise
- know exactly who you market is
- provide them with the exact expert information they want,
- design your content effectively,
- format and present your content following science based guidelines,
- organize yourself to be efficient, effective, and pro-active,
- reach your markets with the multi-marketing system,
- continue to grow personally and professionally.

...then you will succeed!

Chapter Ten

Become the Top Specialist in Your Niche

"Join, Learn New, and Do Good"

Purposes

It is critical that you stay current in your field given this fast moving age. Technology, innovation and digital communications are driving enormous changes in the healthcare industry. Today science is not only discovering revolutionary interventions and treatments but also futuristic systems, processes and approaches. There are a number of ways we can stay ahead of the competition and nurture our passion and professional fulfillment.

If you are an individual practitioner you will especially need sources of support, advice, and socialization. There are several opportunities for you meet these needs.

Coach Yourself

Constantly assess who you are and what you need professionally. A systematic process will ensure that you maintain your passion and motivation.

Here are some key questions to ask yourself:
1. If you were your client, would you re-hire yourself?
2. If someone else had your problem, how would you handle it for them?
3. What haven't you been able to provide for your client or audiences to date?

4. What competencies do you need to develop?
5. What new professionals (or groups) should you be hanging with?

As in the Market Assessment section, I keep a pad and pen next to my bed, favorite chair, dinner table, in my car, and especially in my locker at the gym. Some of my best ideas have come during my workouts. I love all gadgets and own two digital voice recorders (DVR) and have a DVR app on my I-Phone.

- Try to log one new idea a day.
- Keep only one document entitled "New Ideas." Set up sections in the document for each new topic or document you hope to finish in the future. By having only one document you will manage that old "ideas file" a lot easier than the old way.
- Produce something every day. Even it's only a tweet – do it.
- Add or change one concept a day to your current topics or products. Creativity is fluid.

Back to the Future

Now that you have developed your core speeches, and re-purposed your expertise, you now can review your past professional activities. What other related speeches, trainings, writings etc... have you in archives? What is already developed from your past jobs that you could re-write and update and market? "There is gold in them there hills" – so mine it!

Forming a Mastermind Group

Napoleon Hill first suggested the idea of a "master mind" group in his book *Think and Grow Rich.* A master mind group is when two or more individuals meet in a supportive environment to cooperate in accomplishing a common goal, activity, or result. Think of this group as your own Board of Directors. In this group you also then serve as a director for other member's practice or business.

The goal, activity, and result of each group member are to help each other to grow your businesses.

Form a group:

- consider limiting the group to no more than five members.
- get approval from current members before inviting new candidates urgent.
- have each new candidate attend on a temporary basis until the group agrees on permanent status.
- eliminate the possibility of having direct competitors in the group or a conflict of interest in similar markets or niches.

The number and length of the sessions:

- Groups can meet once a month (especially within close geographical areas) or even meet quarterly if the group comes together from throughout the country.
- Groups that meet monthly might meet 2-3 hours while the national groups might meet for a whole weekend, including socialization and downtime.
- Additionally communications between sessions might be desired – whether it is conference call, email or other means.
- The number of members should generally be between 4 and 6 members. The main concern is that during the sessions each member be given enough time for describing their issues and needs, and also allow adequate time for feedback and suggestions from the group. There should be clear understanding on the profile and background of each member. An agreement should also exist regarding when members are allowed to join the group.

Clear purpose(s)

- It is critical that the format, process, and expectation be communicated and agreed by all at the onset.

Examples of clear ground rules:

- Commitment – totally clear to all regarding vision and process of group
- Attendance – how many sessions can be missed
- Confidentiality – regarding business

Consider one or all of these purposes:

- Develop professional relationship(s)
- Obtain resources; fresh perspectives
- Establish accountability from group regarding your goals
- You serve as resource/evaluator/advisor for other group members
- Provide professional skills orientation

Consider setup and structure:

- One set time each month
- Rotate locations
- Establish starting and ending time
- Two hours in length
- Time keeper and secretary - rotate each month
- Structures agenda and ground rules
- Discuss and agree upon a supportive and confidential environment
- Four to six members
- Minutes distributed by email within one week

Mentoring

Mentor at least one person. There is always someone who needs a hand up and can use your guidance in pursuing their professional goals. Share some of your expertise and experience. I mentor at least one person at a time for generally a 3 to 4 month period. The goal is to accomplish at a least one specific outcome.

Some considerations for you in the mentoring process are:
- Be a good listener
- Be supportive
- Have their interest at heart
- Set measurable goals and outcomes
- Provide objective feedback
- Hold the mentee accountable
- Keep track of their mission and vision

The Core Networking Tool

There are two famous adages in business. "There is nothing more powerful in sales than word of mouth," and "The key to effective marketing is relationships." In my business more than fifty per cent of my business comes from referrals and repeat clients. The other fifty per cent comes from my connections and relationships in the healthcare industry.

Arrange as many networks and relationships as you can. The more you cast your net, the more successful and enjoyable your business will be. Network everywhere.

Joining Professional and Industry Associations

Consider the advantage you have professionally to network with a number of professional groups representing each of your competencies. There are professional groups for managing your speaking business, learning how to give speeches, consulting, meeting planning, and your technical, clinical, and medical areas. There are national, state, and local (chapters) divisions. Most local groups meet monthly, state and national groups meet 2 to 3 times a year. All associations have web sites, chat rooms, and sub-specialty educational forums. These groups are member driven and exist for you. Take advantage of online help, archives, and links to other associations and resource sites.

You have a number of opportunities and benefits available from these professional associations:

- Collegial relationships
- Technical learning
- Socialization
- To become involved in the management and activities of the group. You can serve on a committee or the board of directors.
- Ask all your friends and colleagues for contacts in their associations and groups. Send them your one sheet and/or your contact information.
- Stay current in industry trends. This will help you stay up with the latest evidence based information and licensed in your core profession.

Using Social Media

As of this writing, Facebook, Linkedin, and Twitter are the three top web based social networking sites. They allow you to focus even more on the web networks that are the core of speaking professions. Join other professional chat rooms, educational groups and blogs that will relate to you. This type of networking will increase your business. Subscribe to free on-line newsletters and alerts.

Building Your Credentials

Many of your professional associations provide an updated set of competencies for you to assess your current practice. Check with them for availability.

Strive to be credentialed by the prime professional organization in your area of expertise. Strive for higher level certificates and licenses in your core profession. Grow with the industry – stay current.

Be an Expert Practitioner

It doesn't hurt to keep working on a per diem basis in your core specialty while as you are speaking and consulting. This gives you an immense amount of credibility and keeps your ear to the ground for subtle changes in your core profession.

Developing Competencies

Besides your core expert area competencies, consider developing higher level skills in other areas:

- Speaking and consulting competencies
- Technology - for the real geek in you check out "switched.com" for updates on all electronics. We have two

interests in this pursuit: we deal with people and are in the information business.

Interpersonal Communications

Remain professional at all times. It is important that you handle all persons and situations effectively and appropriately. Speaking situations and personalities will challenge your professionalism.

Business Communication Skills

Your presentation is your best business card. You sell you. If your platform skills are not effective then you will lose potential business in your audiences.

Listening skills are really interpersonal skills. Plus you can gather information as you listen.

As a professional speaker no matter how you feel physically, emotionally or psychologically, you always need to rise to the cause when you are in front of your audience.

The Importance of Developing Sales Skills

It is critical that you understand, and are able to implement the fundamentals of selling. How do you:

- Find new sources of clients and speaking venues
- Approach or contact them.
- Use the techniques of making the sale
- Establish and maintain professional relationships

Be an Expert Negotiator

Negotiating is the process of proposing a "valued unique proposition" to the client or audience and they in turn complete the purchase to your satisfaction. Your job as a marketer is to eliminate as many barriers as possible to make the sale. Your role as speaker is to remove as many barriers as possible to deliver the value to the client or audience. It is that simple.

Develop Advanced Presentation Skills

- Group Management – whether it be a crowd of 1000 or a group of two – fun and strategic tricks to control and channel your audiences to the session goals

- Humor – effective use
- Storytelling – components of structuring your signature and other stories
- Interactive Skills – could include magic tricks, card tricks, juggling, singing or dancing

Science Skills to learn

- Andragogy – science of teaching adults
- Platform skills – how to persuade and/or entertain and/or educate your audience at a masters level

- Teaching Techniques – the specific ten steps in developing and delivering behavioral change content
- Survey Techniques – identifying clients, audiences and industry trends and needs
- Questioning Techniques – using the Socratic method for sales, consulting, coaching, counseling, or presenting

To be a successful speaker and consultant in healthcare you must also be balanced in all aspects of your life.

Personal Relaxation Techniques

Stay healthy: physically, mentally, emotionally, and spiritually. *The Guidelines of Preventive Medicine* is a book that needs to be on your shelf. It lists the recommendations to prevent injury and disease by gender and age. These recommendations are the latest evidence based findings from the medical research community.

Another great resource for holistic health is the series of books by Dr Herbert Benson, the least of not being the best seller *Relaxation Response.*

If you are as excited about developing your speaking practice as I am you probably have all the mental stimulation you need. But still consider taking a break by exercising, going to a movie, shopping, or hit that hiking trail. If you don't have a hobby, get one that is not related to your speaking practice. Make it a point to schedule short period of relaxation daily. It is important to balance your day and /or week.

Give to Community Organizations

Give back to the community, network, and socialize all in one stroke. Service, fraternal and religious organizations are usually non-profit, mutual aid organization made up of volunteers that conduct activities to benefit members and their communities. Community is defined as a group of individuals with interrelated needs. Each year these groups deliver over 90 million hours of volunteer service and spend nearly $400 million of charitable programming. As a local member you are able to socialize, give back to the community, and make local business contacts. Many of these organizations are national and allow you a forum to speak anywhere you travel as well as develop national business and social contacts. Provide informational Services to the Community Success is not stagnant. In order to evolve in your profession you must be fluid.

People who are vibrant and passionate are constantly exploring all situations and conditions in life for answers. Explore many other groups that you don't belong to and speak to share new material you are developing. You never know where your next profitable service or product will come from. Providing community service helps to balance your life. Approach the many churches, synagogues, civic or neighborhood associations, fraternal organization, and charities in your area.

Dennis's System at a Glance

I wish you great success towards building and promoting your speaking and consulting practice. I stand ready to help you in any way I can. Please visit my web site www.dennismahoney.org and sign up my free newsletter. This will allow you to contact me and keep in touch along your journey. My first gift to you is the following "Dennis's System at a Glance", divided by skill areas. Use this as a guide to either develop your business plan, skill sets, strategic business or promotional plan. Modify the components to track your projects and outcomes. Good Luck!

Chapter One –Lifestyle

Find your purpose – answer the six questions
Embrace Success
Assess your Willingness answer the five questions
Assess your Ability – answer the four questions
Review Vickery chart and the prevention model matrix
Fill in the prevention model matrix
List the key benefits to you as a professional speaker
List the key motivators for you to grow your speaking practice
Write an ideal lifestyle statement

Chapter One – Appraisals

Perform the twelve step career appraisal
Write the prose "niche" summary statement
Perform the eight personal appraisal questions
List the eight "must" factors for your new lifestyle
Declare your niche
Answer the eight questions to declare your expertise
Write your obituary

Chapter Two – Don't Guess - Assess

Characterize your market(s)
Collect primary, secondary, and trend data
Buy "ask" domain name
Setup "ask" web page
DESIGN YOUR ASSESSMENT TOOLS
1. Oral, 2. Written, 3. Electronic, 4. Combinations
Implement the surveys
1. Interviews
2. Written
3. Electronic

Store the data
Tabulate the data
Analyze the data
Establish metrics
Validate your niche
Write your summary report
Design your brand
Identify Your Unique Value Proposition (UVP)
Setup a continuous surveying system
Establish Google Alerts
Turn ideas into a system

Chapter Three Give Them What They Want

RECONFIRM YOUR PASSION
CLARIFY EXPERTISE
VISUALIZE YOUR MARKET(S) AND THEIR ABILITY TO PAY
Reconfirm your niche
Finish your brand design
Choose one or more "heal the pain"
Identify saleable purpose(s)
List leverage options
Research content
Write

Chapter Three Give Them What They Want

Score your "Andragogy" awareness
Incorporate Blooms and Knowles technology into your presentation
Format
• 1-2 Hour Keynote
• One hour breakout
• ½ -one day seminar and workshops
• Teleconference
• Webinar
• Video conference
• Bootcamp
• Coaching
• Book
• Tips-booklet
• Tips sheet
• Manual
• E-books
• Systems
• Home study program
• Eight digital options
• Membership site
• Bundle options
• Affiliations
• Partnerships
• Sub-contracting arrangements
• Sponsorships

• Distributorships
• Licensing agreements
• Certification program with an educational institutions

Chapter Six – Consult as You Speak

Identify your benefits
Confirm limitations and desirability of venues
Consider types of clients
Identify potential services and products to offer
Develop consulting skills
Design proposal templates
Design agreements and contract templates
Determine fee structure

Chapter Seven – Manage Your Business

Plan and Build Your Best Practice
Design Your Business Model
Determine the scope of your practice
Write your mission and vision statements
Plan Your Business
Build and Manage Your Systems
• Office
• Staffing
• Legal
• Finance
• Audit
Organize your professional management schedule
Identify your potential barriers to success
Incorporate techniques to control attitudes and emotions
Identify your personal stressors
Customize an effective stress management and coping technique program
Apply the principles of time management to your personal and professionals activities

Chapter Nine – It is All About Marketing

Implement the public relations chart instruments
Include the "Fifteen Future Funders" into your promotion campaign
Promote your practice using the eight advertising steps
Incorporate: the eight personal and personnel advertising vehicles
Incorporate the seven professional material vehicles
Promote your practice with CDs and/or DVDs
Utilize **The Eight Electrifying Sales Efforts in your sales activities**
Become expert at listening skills and overcoming resistance
Define the purpose of your pitch
Consider incorporating the seventeen sales tips in your strategic promotion plan
Hire a graphic artist
Design a logo
Obtain a head shot
Hire a web master and a Host
Develop a blog, tweet, link, and "friend"
Initiate social marketing channels
Hire an email service provider
Optimize your presence on the internet
Write a comprehensive strategic marketing plan

Section Nine - Professional Development

Develop a self-coaching plan
Join a master mind group
Mentor someone
Network
• Professional and industry associations
• Professional chat rooms
• "Google alerts"
• Social media sites
Re-assess your credentials
Develop new competencies
Advance your presentation skills
Form new hobbies, and social outlets
Provide service to your communities

Opportunities to Grow Your Business

Visit www.dennismahoney.org to:

- ✓ Sign up for Dennis's free "Strategy Boosters"

- ✓ Have Dennis join Your Book Club or Mastermind meeting

- ✓ Join Dennis's Speakers workshops

- ✓ Work with Dennis from Your Own "Home Study Program"

- ✓ Join Dennis for a Teleconference

- ✓ Train with Dennis at a weekend Bootcamp

- ✓ Let Dennis know what else you need (www. askdennismahoney.com)

SUGGESTED READINGS

Bolles, Richard N., *What Color Is Your Parachute, A Practical Manual for Job Hunters and Career Changers*, 40th edition, (Ten Speed Press, Berkeley, California, 2012)

Burchard, Brendon, *The Millionaire Messenger*, (The Burchard Group, New York, 2011)

Carter, Judy, *The Comedy Bible*, (Fireside: New York, 2001)

Herman, Jeff and Deborah Levin Herman, *Write The Perfect Book Proposal,* 2nd edition, (Wiley, New York, 2001)

Kennedy, Dan S., *The Ultimate Sales Letter*, 3rd edition, (Adams Media Corporation, Avon Massachusetts, 2006)

Kremer, John, *1001 Ways To Market Your Books,* 6th edition, (Open Horizon, , Taos New Mexico, 2008)

Krum Cindy, *Mobile Marketing, Finding Your Customers No Matter Where They Are*, (Pearson Education Inc., Indianapolis, 2010)

Lutze, Heather, *The Findability Formula, The Easy Non-Technical Approach to Search Engine Marketing*, (Wiley, Hoboken, New Jersey, 2009)

Miller, William R. and Stephen Rollnick, *Motivational Interviewing, Preparing People for Change,* 2nd edition, (Guilford Press, New York, 2003)

Poynter, Dan, *The Self-Publishing Manual, How to Write, Print and Sell Your Own Book,* 14th edition, (Para Publishing, Santa Barbara, 2009)

Ross, Marilyn, and Sue Collier. *The Complete Guide to Self-Publishing, 5th* edition. 2010

Rutledge, Patrice-Anne, *Teach Yourself Linkedin in 10 Minutes,* (SAMA, Indianapolis, 2010)

Sampson, Brent, *Sell Yourself on Amazon*, (Outskirts Press, Denver, 2007)

Thomases, Hollis, *Twitter Marketing in One Hour*, (Wiley: Indianapolis, 2010)

Weiss, Alan, *Million Dollar Consulting*, 4th edition, (McGraw-Hill, New York, 2009)

Winget, Larry, *You're Broke Because You Want To Be*, Penquin Books, New York, 2010)

CPSIA information can be obtained at www.ICGtesting.com
Printed in the USA
LVOW05s1918290713

345204LV00025B/817/P